What is Neurotheology?

What is Neurotheology?

Brian C. Alston

Visit www.booksurge.com to order additional copies.

What is Neurotheology?

Table of Contents

INTRODUCTION

The history of thought is often perceived as a gradual transition from spiritual explanations of the reality and human being to material or scientific ones. Though oversimplified, such perception is true to certain extent: science absolutely dominates modern world, while spiritual explanations of the reality have lost their former credibility. The recent interest to the non-material phenomena is an encouraging sign that such state of things will soon become obsolete. These days humanity have recently reached the point at which the necessity to widen the notions and concepts of science that traditionally cover the domain of material world to the non-material domain is obvious.

Traditionally, the human mind, spirituality, beliefs and ideas have not been considered by western science. Partially, it was due to lack of proper methods and techniques applicable to study the mind and non-material phenomena; partially due to specific philosophic paradigms underlying the scientific approach. Contemporary science lacks tools and methodologies to be applied in studies of non-physical phenomena. For example, no existing scientific discipline is capable of explaining the influence of beliefs—the core stem of the mind—on our thoughts, feelings and experience. A series of disciplines has emerged to fill this vacuum with neurotheology taking the lead in the scientific study of brain, mind and belief phenomena.

This essay focuses upon the application of neuroscience to studying religious and spiritual beliefs. However, other sciences like cognitive science, biology, genetics, chemistry and psychology also apply their tools to study beliefs other than religious and spiritual. Neurochemistry, neurophilosophy, neuroeconomics and neuropolitics are examples of this tendency when neuroscientific tools and findings are applied to improve our understanding of problems or issues within the existing discipline.

One of such recent and interesting perspectives on brain, mind, and belief establishes the connection between mind and matter through epigenetics. Bruce Lipton, the most renowned representative of this approach, maintains that neither genes per se nor DNA determine who we are: it is the cell and its membrane that regulates its contact with its environment. Lipton postulates humans have direct influence over that environment through nutrition, the energy of our thoughts and the conviction of our beliefs[1].

Gene-based theories of spirituality represent another approach to relate brain, mind, and belief. Thus, Dean Hamer maintains that faith is hardwired into our genes. Hamer supposes that the spirituality phenomena are determined by a combination of several different genes plus specific environmental influences that play equally important role[2].

The key issue in understanding the broader project of neurotheology is the nature of beliefs—the central mental constructs of human being that shape the core of human personality and identity. The most distinct characteristic of beliefs is their variance: there are cultural and social, religious and scientific, political and economic, ethical and historical and other types of beliefs. This paper focuses upon the application of neuroscience to studying religious and spiritual beliefs. The attempt to relate neuroscience and religion is only one instance of neurotheology's application: it exemplifies the broader scope of neurotheology as a budding discipline aiming to make good on the current claim of science in various fields.

Although theology and science represent two strikingly different and conflicting fields of knowledge, an attempt to marry them may be not as hopeless as one may think. The key issue is to correctly understand the meaning and purpose of this attempt. Neurotheology should not be perceived as a narrow isolated discipline attempting to establish the missing link between the human being and God. Despite the focus of contemporary neurotheological research on the study of brain and religious/spiritual experiences such as meditation and prayer, this approach to studying brain, mind and beliefs can also be employed by other sciences.

Neurotheology is an emerging discipline that seeks to integrate two vastly different perspectives—scientific and theological—into one broad field of knowledge and to provide an appropriate framework and methodological basis to join these varying perspectives together. Development of neurotheology as an independent branch of knowledge is a daring attempt to establish multidisciplinary perspective that may potentially facilitate further studies of each separate discipline included in it. The core idea underlying this attempt is to find out the way in which science and its tools can contribute to better understanding of theology, mind and spirituality and visa versa[3].

Some recent neuroscientific findings suggest that from the beginning of conscious live, the human brain searches for visual signs that conform to an understanding of reality present at inception. Modern imaging studies reveal physiological responses of the brain to stimuli perceived through the five senses. Other studies pinpoint brain areas stimulation of which produces the same effects which are otherwise achieved through prayer or mediation[4]. These studies have drawn attention to a number of highly complicated questions concerning the origin of religion and spiritual phenomena, the relationship between brain and mind, the nature of God, etc. Neurotheology advances as a nouveau discipline aiming to make good on the recent findings of neuroscience by relating the paradigms of theology and science.

Aldous Huxley is thought to be the first to use the term neurotheology in a philosophical or pseudoscientific context. In his utopian novel Island, published in 1962, Huxley mentions neurotheology alongside with such disciplines as pharmacology, sociology, physiology, autology, metachemistry and mycomysticism[5]. The first usage of the new term in a scientific context is normally attributed to James Ashbrook, the outstanding American scientist, and his 1984 article titled "*Neurotheology: The Working Brain and the Work of Theology*"[6].

Although Eugene D'Aquili began the research on brain and spiritual experiences in the 1960s, the first systematic attempts to relate neuroscience to spirituality and belief phenomena can be traced back to 1970s-1980s. James Ashbrook, Michael Persinger, Eugene D'Aquili, Charles Laughlin, and other researchers employed the new tools of neuroscience to expose neuropsychological determinants of ritual behavior, reveal specific psychological characteristics of human beings, and define dominance of the right or left brain hemisphere in relation to various patterns of belief and images of the divine[7]. Ashbrook used the new term to label precisely this type of scientific enquiry.

The term *neurotheology* reflects the idea of strong biological basis underlying spiritual experiences of human being. Sporadically, a number of publications on the neural basis of religious and spiritual experiences have been printed over the 1990's—first half of the 2000's. In 1994 the American Institute for Mindfulness published *Neurotheology—Virtual Religion in the 21st Century* by Laurence O. McKinney[8]. This publication addressed the status and position of neurotheology within the context of traditional sciences. In 2002, Rhawn Joseph edited a series of 38 articles in his book *Neurotheology: Brain, Science, Spirituality, Religious Experience*. The articles covered a series of topics ranging from religious beliefs and spirituality to methodological peculiarities of scientific perspectives, such as neuroscience and psychology[9].

The last decade of 20th century was marked by increasing interest toward the so-called 'God-spot' phenomena. The interest was ignited by a series of publications attempting to reveal the mystical relationship between the human brain and spirituality with the help of brain-imaging data collected from Tibetan Buddhists in the state of meditation and praying Franciscan monks[10]. The advanced technology of brain imaging allowed the researchers to pinpoint the areas of the human brain responsible for the experience of religious transcendence thus proving existence of physiological basis for spiritual phenomena.

Yet, neurotheology goes further than providing a mere affirmation of the assumption that spiritual experiences of human beings have neural basis: "By pinpointing the brain areas involved in spiritual experiences and tracing how such experiences arise, the scientists hope to learn whether anyone can have such experiences, and why spiritual experiences have the qualities they do"[11]. Advanced methods and techniques employed by neuroscience (e.g. brain mapping and brain imaging) provide the scientists with clear picture of how the human brain responds to stimulation of our senses and reveal functional differences of various brain regions.

MAIN DISCUSSION

For thousands of years numbers of great thinkers and philosophers have attempted to grasp the essence of relationship between human being and the higher power, understand the nature of God and spirituality and define the position of human being in the universe. The search for seemingly unknowable resulted in abundant definitions of the nature of God, sophisticated discourses on the relationship between the God and human, rationalizing existence of supernatural power, etc. Later, these issues turned even more sophisticated and controversial due to development of science as an empirical paradigm of perception and knowledge.

Although the scientific discovery and religious faith are still perceived as conflicting paradigms, history records a numbers of efforts to reconcile science and religion. Perhaps, the most consequential and successful effort to reconcile science and religion was made by Thomas Aquinas (1225-1274), the Catholic Church's foremost philosopher and theologian, back in the 13th century. Aquinas believed that the existence of God can be 'proved' via application of reasoning to prove the value of faith. Aquinas' incorporated Aristotelian thinking into his views and managed to force the theologians of his days apply the concept of scientific rationalism to their reasoning: "Reconciling the Augustinian emphasis upon the human spiritual principle with the Averroist claim of autonomy for knowledge derived from the senses, Aquinas insisted that the truths of faith and those of sense experience, as presented by Aristotle, are fully compatible and complementary"[12].

Aquinas maintained that knowledge, including the knowledge of God, originated in sensation and can only be made intelligible by the action of the intellect. Human being is a 'composite substance' consisting of a rational soul and body which are linked closely to each other: the rational soul is spiritual, while body is a subsistent form of the soul. Correspondingly, the soul confers all sensitive and intellectual capacity with the human mind dependent in this life on the human body; the mind, in its turn, has the unique capacity for abstracting and forming ideas through sense perception. Therefore, human knowledge of God and reality is always mediated through what is not God, created order and created minds[13]. Later, other approaches such as Natural Theology and Cosmology aimed at reconciliation of the religious and scientific paradigms as well.

The roots of contemporary issues in relating religion and science can be traced back to the early philosophical polemics on mind/body and spirit/matter issue, which still remains arguably the most popular topic in modern philosophy. There are two time-honored philosophical positions: *monism* rooted in teaching of pre-Socratic philosophers (Shankara, Pythagoras, Heraclitus, etc) and Neo-Platonist school (Plotinus) and *dualism* exemplified by Plato, Aristotle, Hume, Kant, Heidegger and Descartes.

Monism comprises two major schools of thought about the relation between the mental and the physical: *nomological monism* or materialism and *anomalous monism*. Donald Davidson was the first to propose the thesis of *anomalous monism* claiming it was the solution to the mind body problem[14]. This thesis asserts a dualism of properties maintaining that it is misleading to speak of the mental as against the physical rather than the mental as against the neural[15].

René Descartes (1596-1650), the French mathematician, philosopher, and physiologist, adopted dualistic views on mind/body relationship claiming that conscious minds exist on a separate, non-physical level[16]. Descartes located the soul in the pineal gland, the only symmetrical organ in the brain without a left and right counterpart, thus raising the question of the relationship of mind to the brain and nervous system[17]. By emphasizing radical distinctions between body and mind, Descartes initiated the ongoing mind/body polemic in western philosophy and science.

One of the reasons for the ongoing debate on the mind/body issue is abundance of theoretical arguments and theories coupled with lack of empirical evidences and effective methodological basis. Neurotheology seeks to close this gap and finally answer the inquiries concerning the nature of the human brain (physical nature vs. spirituality), specific functionality of various brain areas, physiological basis of spirituality and others.

Human brain is the most complex organ of human body. Although recent advances in neuroscience have elucidated certain aspects of its functioning the comprehensive picture of the brain will hardly be available for decades to come. Recent research contends that the human brain contains approximately one hundred billion cells (neurons) with one hundred trillion connections between them[18]. While defining the number of neurons and neuron connection in the human brain is comparatively simple task, studying the brain in action has been the pot of gold at the end of the rainbow until recently. Emergence and rapid advancement of neurotechnology made it possible to accomplish this task. Functional Magnetic Resonance Imaging (fMRI), Positron Emission Tomography (PET) and Single Photon Emission Computed Tomography (SPECT) provide perspectives on the brain and it's functioning with living subjects.

Establishing associations between certain brain areas and specific abilities/behaviors has become the focus of neuroscientific research. The human brain consists of two hemispheres, right and left—this basic characteristic is known to anyone. Yet, although the brain functions as an integral system recent studies involving application of advanced neuroscientific techniques has confirmed different functional specialization of the hemispheres. Specialization of the right hemisphere includes situational logic, imagination and analytical processing of perceived information. The major function of this hemisphere is to create patterns of meaning. By contrast, the left hemisphere is specialized in acquisition and development of language and using it to interpret and explain various experiences processed by the right hemisphere[19].

A series of studies conducted over the last two decades revealed even more striking findings. Techniques applied by the researchers roughly fall into two types: studying brain activity with the help of brain imaging techniques in order to identify the brain regions which change or stimulating spiritual experience with drugs.

Over the late 1970s-1980s Dr. Michael Persinger performed several experimental studies sending low-strength, rotating magnetic pulses to the amygdala, the hippocampus, and the caudate nucleus. Stimulation of these areas caused Persinger's subjects to feel a variety of spiritual experiences including dream-like hallucinations, visions, out-of-body experiences, altered states of consciousness and a spectral presence in the room[20]. Persinger explained the results assuming that left hemisphere of the subjects interpreted the right hemisphere as a separate "sensed presence", also perceived as the higher power or God[21].

A seizure study of epileptic patients conducted by researchers at the University of California in San Diego in 1997 found out that one effect of the patients' seizures was escalation of their involuntary response to words associated with faith or religion[22]. The patients suffering from an unusual form of epilepsy were then compared with non-epileptic patients in similarly designed studies only to discover similar results. The area identified as the "God-spot", is located behind the temples, temporal lobe: when it is stimulated patients report experiencing a variety of mystical experience including seeing God[23]. However, the researchers pointed out that this uncovering in no way suggested that religion was simply a matter of brain chemistry: the results rather provided a level of explanation of what brain regions may be involved.

Leaning upon the research findings of Roger W. Sperry (split-brain research) and David H. Hubel and Torsten N. Wiesel (the nature of specific visual response patterns), James Ashbrook and Carol R. Albright postulate two basic presumptions defining the inter-workings of the human brain: humans are "....object-seeking and meaning-making creatures"[24].

Sperry's research of split-brain patients suggests that the human brain tends to derive meaning from all it experiences[25]. In a study involving a 16-year-old boy with severed inter-hemisphere connections, Sperry used two images: a hen and a winter snow scene. These images were presented to the boy in such a fashion the image of hen reached only the left hemisphere and the image of a winter snow scene reached only the right one. After Sperry presented the teenager a series of 8 representations and asked him to choose the one image best matching each of the previously presented images.

The subject correctly pointed to a shovel which corresponded to the snow scene and a chicken head. However, when Sperry asked him about the reasons for his choice, the boy gave the following response, "'Oh, that's easy. The chicken goes with the chicken head and you need a shovel to clean out the chicken shed"[26]. Due to functional specifics of the left hemisphere, the teenager correctly established the connection between the image featuring hen and the chicken head. However, the severance of the subject's inter-hemisphere neural pathway did not allow the left hemisphere to access the perceptions developed by the right hemisphere[27]. Despite the lack of knowledge, the subject's left hemisphere attempted to infer a connection between what it had indirectly witnessed (via the hand motion) and what it knew directly. Ashbrook and Albright reasonably suggested that the human brain possesses an innate need to create meaning and forge relationships amongst external stimuli: this became the founding stone of their neurological model.

Hubel and Wiesel assumed that each species has its own unique visual limitations. These limitations result in substantial variance in perception of external reality[28]. In a series of studies involving frogs Hubel and Wiesel found out that a moving object, a moving object entering the field of vision and then stopping, a decrease in illumination, and a dark spot "shifting against a dark and light background"[29] were the only visual stimuli that drew a response in the subjects' neural system[30].

Further studies involving newborns led Hubel and Wiesel to the following findings:

- 'a face-like pattern elicits a greater extent of [newborn] tracking behavior than does a non-face-like pattern'
- Newborns focus the longest on complex visual stimuli[31].

On the basis of these findings Ashbrook and Albright theorize that "...the evolutionary yearnings of the human mind find manifestation in the idea of the Christian God"[32]. The intrinsic need to know (cognitive imperative) makes humans attribute meaning and purpose to a "higher power" when such evidence is missing within the natural environment. Ashbrook and Albright claim this need to be exclusively anthropomorphic: humans are the only biological species that is innately driven to search for its likeness. Moreover, driven by the anthropomorphic inclination to search for complexity, humans tend to compare the higher power to the human being attributing to the latter the incomprehensible degree of complexity[33].

Drawing upon neuroscientist Paul MacLean's partition of the brain into three evolutionary episodes (the reptilian, the mammalian and the neocortex), Ashbrook and Albright emphasize correlations between the functional value of each brain structure and "God's way of being God."[34] The existence of such correlations would definitely allow asserting the relationship between the God and the brain.

MacLean's partition reflects each evolutionary episode in the physical makeup of the brain and maps the behaviors associated with those brain regions. Thus, the earliest or reptilian portion of the brain is most involved with autonomic regulation and basic survival skills. The mammalian brain, associated with the limbic system, plays a primary role in emotional responses and memory. The neocortex is strongly associated with language, reasoning and attention[35].

Neurological findings demonstrate that Ashbrook and Albright's hypothesis is at least partially valid. Studies involving reptiles that do not have the mammalian and neocortex brain structures demonstrate a territoriality and hierarchical emphasis that probably corresponds to a "God who belongs to God's creatures...[and is understood] as the highest of all"[36]. Correspondingly, the concept of God "as interactive and nurturing, among others, allegedly reflects the human capacity for empathy and the urge to relate conferred by the inner workings of the limbic system"[37].

Ashbrook and Albright further elaborated the basic principles of the new approach toward understanding and studying the relationship between the human brain and spiritual experiences. These principles can be summarized as follows:

- Possibility of viewing neuroscience as linking partner between science and theology/spirituality;
- Possibility of a "God-spot" in the brain;
- Explanations of human behavior and experience through brain mapping.

From this perspective emotions may be the key to understanding spiritual experience. The limbic system, including the hypothalamus, amygdala, and hippocampus, assign emotional value to all incoming stimuli. In MacLean's classification the three basic brain sections of the limbic system are located in the area of the brain that exerts serious influence on the autonomic nervous system. The limbic system places survival of the individual above all else. The "sense of self" created by this "ego-centered" interpretation, i.e., survival interpretation, comprises the bio-chemical energy that holds the ego-matrix together[38].

Neuroscientist Andrew Newberg suggests that the primitive interpretive function of the limbic system is ego-oriented. Consequently, humans are placed within the dyadic (good vs. bad) mode of interpreting reality. Newberg argues that there are two central cognitive operators which function together in the brain/mind process of transforming incoming stimuli into reality. The causal operator is involved in identifying and processing the causes of incoming stimuli in the moment-by-moment flow of consciousness, while the binary operator arranges the incoming stimuli into a sort of order opposing them: "This interpretive function of brain/mind draws from the most primitive parts of the brain, interprets data on a survival continuum, and is decidedly dualistic"[39].

The simplest application of the binary operator function is navigating through the material world: it allows us to distinguish between left and right, up and down, back and forth. When dealing with non-material abstract concepts the binary operator creates polar opposites which carry important emotional signals. In this case the operator's function drives us to create dualistic cognitive structures to explain the experiences of life, death, misery. Newberg views this process as the basis for all human mythic/religious activity[40].

Also located in the inferior parietal lobe, the binary operator allows humans to extract meaning from the external world by ordering abstract elements into dyads[41]. Dyads include good and evil, right and wrong, justice and injustice, happy and sad, heaven and hell, internal and external, human and divine. Dyads can also involve setting up and placing in opposition beings such as God and Satan. Within dyads each opposite derives its meaning from its contrast with the other opposite. They are defined in relation to each other, and D'Aquili and Newberg maintain that they are particularly important in the generation of myth. In religion opposites are routinely set against each other and, according to D'Aquili and Newberg, play "a very important role in the generation of our mental picture of reality."[42] The functions of this operator correspond to the first, second and fourth methodologies of neurotheology, personal ultimacy, sacrificial re-birth and inner life.

The prevalence of apocalyptical tradition in various religious systems all over the world is a good example of the join functioning of the causal and binary operators. The basic dualistic interpretation of Us vs. Them strongly affects human behavior and consciousness. This neurologically biased concept, which underlies human consciousness, found its reflection in the religious, political, economic and cultural systems[43].

Drawing upon correlations between the neocortex regions of the brain and the respective visions of "God as relational" and "God as [a] source of order"[44], Ashbrook and Albright also assert that the brain is wired for belief in the higher power. The authors address this perspective as an *emergent holism*: the trend in modern neuroscience that recognizes the relationship between the mind and the brain as a complex dynamic[45].

Various regions of the brain guide the autonomic nervous system of human body. Similarly to any biological species, human being has to interpret sensory stimuli and properly respond to them by making certain decision on vitally important matters: nutrition, shelter and other fundamental needs. The phenomenon of 'mind' emerges as the result of these extraordinarily sophisticated interconnections between the autonomic nervous system and the neocortex, the structure of in the brain that is believed to be responsible for the evolution of human intelligence[46]. Newberg and D'Aquili characterize this system of interconnections as follows: "The brain is a collection of physical structures that gather and process sensory, cognitive, and emotional data; the mind is the phenomenon of thoughts, memories, and emotions that arise from the perceptual processes of the brain"[47].

The doctrine of emergent holism postulates that the brain and mind not only originate the experience, but also mediate it. Neuroscience, in its turn, performs as the mediator between traditional science and theology to facilitate further research of the brain/mind relationship. D'Aquili and Newberg, the brightest representatives of this doctrine, develop a neurotheology from a neuropsychological and evolutionary perspective. While asserting the necessary roles for the brain, central nervous system and mind to religious experience, and human experience in general, the authors avoid reductionism Ashbrook and Albright are prone to by standing open the door to "paradoxical and counterintuitive"[48] experience between human life, the world, pure consciousness or an existent God.

D'Aquili and Newberg argue that the mind and brain form a "mystical union" providing the way humans experience, interpret, generate and mediate religious experience. While focusing on structures most relevant to human experience, emotion, and cognition the authors map how the mind experiences the sacred. Through the research of neuropsychology they identify the biological mechanisms involved and explore areas such as human myth-making, ritual, liturgy and theology. They propose that neurotheology serve as a meta-theology, a neuropsychological basis for the study of human primal patterns in comparative religions[49].

Extrapolating from insightful research by D'Aquili and Newberg this essay proposes three postulates that form the basis for our understanding of neurotheology and enable this discipline to fulfill the role as linking partner between the fields of science and religion.

1. Because science can demonstrate no other place, realm, or mechanism by which the human mind comes about other than the brain, the brain and mind exist in contingent, dynamic relation[50];

2. Because the brain underlies all sense experiences of living human beings, any human religious or spiritual experience is necessarily mediated by the brain[51];

3. Our human tendencies to identify, measure and structure or categorize reality, search for more within and beyond ourselves, and ritualize our existence are all linked in some way to the make-up and function of the brain and mind. Essential features of any and all theologies, spiritual, religious and scientific systems correlate directly with the structure and function of the human brain and mind[52].

These postulates suggest that mind and body interact with each other: our perceptions, thoughts, intentions, volitions, and anxieties directly affect our bodies and our behaviors. States of the brain and nervous system, in their turn, generate our states of mind. However, the general view involves an important contradiction, namely: the brain and nervous system belong to the physical world while thoughts, feelings, consciousness, and other states of mind are part of the mental dimension.

Beliefs and belief systems shape the core stem of the mind. Similarly to the relationship between the brain and the mind, beliefs represent "ontological complexes, demanding complex stories"[53]. The relationship between the physical phenomena, such as behavior, and beliefs can hardly be explained within any existing discipline as well as the influence of beliefs on thoughts, feelings, and experience.

The phenomenon of human behavior traditionally belongs to the realm of psychology, both general and social. The word psychology is of Greek origin, "psyche"—soul, "logos"—learning, and literally means 'the science about human soul'. Till now there is no one integrate science of psychology (like mathematics, for instance); modern psychology represents a conglomerate of different, sometimes exceptive, approaches.

Freud and Charcot were the first scientists whom began systematically observe their patients in order to better understand their behavior. Although their patients were largely psychotics, further research discovered that certain peculiarities of their behavior were characteristic not only to mentally ill patients, but to normal people as well (introversion, extraversion, rigidity, irritation, etc)[54]. The outburst of experimental studies and theoretical discourses on various aspects of human personality and behavior that followed the first uncertain attempts to unveil the secrets of human psycho marked the beginning of the age of psychology.

Atomistic approach that predominated in the beginning of the last century led to a situation when the inner human was relentlessly dissected into hundreds of separate processes, states and conditions. In the end human psycho turned out to be a system of independent psychological functions that could hardly compose an integrate system and failed to explain more or less complex models of social behavior. Famous English psychologist R. Kettel drew a perfect analogy between that situation and staging of "Hamlet" without the Prince of Denmark: everything seemed fine except for only one thing—the main hero[55].

Contemporary state of things in the field of psychology is perfectly summarized by the statement of Jerome Bruner: "no theory can ever be the true theory...there can be no one sole and unitary way of understanding of human nature, its variations, its settings, or its growth"[56]. At present we have a great diversity of psychological approaches focusing upon various aspects of human behavior, personality development, etc. They can be classified depending on various factors: manner of explanation of behavior (dynamic, interactive), way of obtaining data (experimental— non-experimental), age range and others. .

Psychoanalytic theory of Sigmund Freud was the first attempt to create a comprehensive picture of personality and human development. Freud emphasized the crucial role of the early years of childhood. The first six years of the child shape the personality and whatever happens to a person later in life is nothing but "a mere ripple on the surface of a personality structure"[57]. Consequently, the basic idea of psychoanalysis is that behavior is determined by unconscious forces like early childhood experiences and innate drives. Freud also introduced the concept of defense mechanisms explaining and proving their role in determining human behavior and development of personality[58].

Behavioral theory is concerned with the behavior of people, i.e. how people learn to behave in particular ways in particular situations. This approach can equally be termed the learning theory: learning is the main determinant of human behavior. The main concern of behaviorists is establishing a direct association between two events: environmental influence and behavioral response. The perfect example of this linkage is "Pavlov's dog". Behaviorism also denies value of any hidden determinants of human behavior such as instincts, sexual desires, conscious and unconscious inclinations, beliefs and so on[59].

While behaviorists considered human being to be a kind of processor processing external stimuli into behavioral patterns, representatives of cognitive approach focused upon what goes on inside the processor. The way human brain processes, organizes, treats and interprets information is termed the process of cognition[60]. From this perspective human behavior is immanently linked to the individually unique characteristics of the cognition process.

Psychoanalysis made people slaves of their unconscious desires, behaviorism turned them into biological robots hardly distinguished from animals, but only humanistic psychology liberated them by admitting human beings possess consciousness. Humans were announced entirely different from all other organisms due to their capability to interfere with the course of their existence and determine their behavior through conscious choices[61]. Humanistic psychologists (including *Gestalt* or field theory) were the first to adopt a genuinely holistic approach to human personality: they viewed the human condition as one integrative unity, something more than a mere sum of the physical, social and psychological characteristics[62].

And finally, biopsychology focuses upon the impact of the brain and neurotransmitter functions on thoughts, feelings and behavior. In fact, this approach represents an attempt to marry basic psychology to neuroscience. Biopsychologists are interested in how physiological mechanisms affect the process of cognitions, emotional responses and other functions of the brain[63].

The variety of psychological schools and approaches seem to cover absolutely all aspects of human psycho and behavior. However, neither perspective provides a comprehensive approach to study the internal and external qualities of belief phenomena and fully reveal their influence on behavior of human beings. Only some major theories address this issue, though partially: they provide a limited framework encompassing only certain types of beliefs (e.g. stereotypes, attitudes, schemas, etc.), and leaving other belief perspectives on the sideway. Cognitive science, psychological theory of William James, psychoanalytic teaching of Freud and, probably, behavioral therapy of Albert Ellis belong to this thin group. The theory of archetypes developed by Carl Jung, Karen Horney and their followers is also believed to provide the link between the material and spiritual worlds[64].

WHAT IS NEUROTHEOLOGY?

Emergence of Neurotheology is an attempt to close the existing gap by providing a balanced framework to study how the brain and mind experience, interpret, generate, and mediate belief phenomena. The new discipline serves as a collaborative approach between a range of sciences to explain and interpret the connections between beliefs and belief systems to thought, feeling, behavior, and experience. Neurotheology accomplishes two major objectives:

1. Establish comprehensive, interdisciplinary approaches to understand beliefs.
2. Explain, interpret and predict the influences of beliefs to thought, feeling, behavior and experience.

The term *neurotheology* is of Greek origin: *neuro* is a common prefix in words for concepts and topics in relation to the brain and central nervous system; *theology* consists of the Greek words θεος (*theos*), "God" and λογος (*logos*), "word" or "reason". However, the meaning of neurotheology tends to be broader than a mere sum of the compound meanings, while the meaning of each constituent term also extends significantly.

Firstly, the term *neuro* refers not only to the central nervous system, but to human physiology in general. Secondly, the term *theology* is used in a broader sense without restricting its meaning to traditional Christian, Judaist or Buddhist context. This broadening is justified by the fact that the origins of classical theological discourses can be traced back to the ancient belief systems and perspectives (e.g. classical Greek mythology, Hellenistic theology, etc.) that can barely be termed religion in contemporary meaning of this word. Therefore, it would be misleading to restrict theology to either religious or spiritual beliefs: it rather refers to beliefs in general.

In traditional psychology belief is "...a representational mental state that takes the form of a propositional attitude"[65]. Although this rather narrow definition helps avoid many difficulties (methodological in the first turn), it seriously limits the initial philosophic meaning of the term *belief*. Philosophically speaking, belief is a conviction to the truth of a proposition without its verification, which characterizes it as a highly subjective concept.

In the religious sense, 'belief' is a segment of a wider spiritual or moral foundation, normally termed 'faith'. Religion has always been one of the most important issues of human life since the dawn of modern civilization. Although history and philosophy provide us with sufficient information to make up an objective opinion on many religion-related issues, the researcher whom attempts to do so inevitably enters the dangerous borderline between the conflicting realms of theology and secular worldview.

Although humans believe in more things than they are able to imagine, beliefs can be classified into two major groups: individual and collective/social. Individual beliefs are represented by assumptions, conclusions, explanations, theories, schemas, states of mind, attitudes, etc. Beliefs are implicit and explicit frameworks that help us make sense of our experiences and serve as the foundation upon which humans build their short-term and long-term expectations. Beliefs and belief systems can also be scientific or psychological, religious or mystical, economic or political, cultural or social with much influence from technology and many ethical implications.

Neurotheology provides eight major dimensions of belief systems each implying distinct approach to explain and interpret the relationship between brain, mind, and belief phenomena to thought, feeling, behavior and experience:

1. Mystical, Religious, Spiritual and Theological Traditions and Experiences;
2. Scientific Programs and Psychological Theories;
3. Historical and Philosophical Traditions;
4. Economic Initiatives;
5. Socio-Political Influences;
6. Cultural Manifestations;
7. Technological Developments;
8. Ethical Implications.

The emerging methodology of neurotheology represents an attempt to marry the empirical nature of science to purely theoretical discourses of theology. The key idea underlying the methodological basis of neurotheology is to identify major dimensions of the discipline, map the possibilities to deal with multiple perspectives on brain, mind and beliefs and offer a way to properly understand and effectively compare research in the field of the new discipline. Currently, four major methodological principles/concepts are employed to achieve this goal providing the basis to unfold and analyze neurotheological phenomena in their complexity. These principles are:

1. Personal Ultimacy (Human Perception of Reality/Worldview/Paradigm);
2. Sacrificial Re-birth (Typologies);
3. Ritual Experience (Habit);
4. Inner life (Interiority).

These methodologies attempt to ensure proper interface between the conflicting realms of science and theology. The interface is available due to application of liberal theological doctrines formulated by the outstanding German thinker of 19th century Friedrich Schleiermacher whom is considered, in many respects, the progenitor of practical theology. Schleiermacher's methodology and theology exerted a deep impact on the development of practical theology as a formal, theological discipline[66]. The philosopher maintained that both religion and science are ways for finite humanity to experience infinite God. The difference between these ways lies only in the way of assessing each: religion is humanly assessable through feeling or sensation and science through knowledge[67].

Being antecedent to beliefs, actions and dogmas, religion is a mingling of the theoretical and the practical. It represents our human "sense and taste for the infinite," involving personal commitment but connecting beyond individual consciousness to a world consciousness encompassing every form of human knowing including science. "Religion is for you at one time a way of thinking, a faith, a particular way of contemplating the world, and of combining what meets us in the world: at another, it is a way of acting, a peculiar desire and love, a special kind of conduct and character. Without this distinction of a theoretical and practical you could hardly think at all, and though both sides belong to religion, you are usually accustomed to give heed chiefly to only one at a time"[68].

Schleiermacher affirms the existence of a third dimensional aspect to human experience, the spirit world, and contends that the spirit world is perhaps more influential on brain and mind than many of the theories correlating brain and mind: "religion is an indispensable 'third' in being human, alongside knowing and doing"[69]. Schleiermacher's methodology, developed on the basis of his practical views on theology, plays an important role in development of the methodological background of neurotheology.

1) Personal Ultimacy

Personal ultimacy is the first methodological concept of neurotheology. This concept defines the human tendency to structure and make sense of reality (both external and internal), name and define our perceptions of sensitive experiences. The core idea of this methodological concept is that neurotheology should relate the basic metaphysical claims of both science and theology establishing new connections and suggesting new interpretations in order to join these varying perspectives together.

A metaphysical system is a type of philosophy or study that uses broad concepts to help define all reality, material and immaterial, subjective and objective, and our understanding of it[70]. Metaphysics treats the most general and fundamental principles underlying all reality and all knowledge and might include the study of the nature of the human mind, the definition and meaning of existence, or the nature of space, God, time, and/or causality, the first causes of things, etc[71].

Metaphysics can serve as a basis for paradigms or world-views. The term paradigm coined by Thomas Kuhn encompasses both the global shared commitments of a scientific group and a particular allotment of commitment or a subset of the global[72]. Paradigms serve as patterns, examples, or models of thought, overall concepts explaining complex processes, ideas, or sets of data. They represent sets of rules and regulations establishing or defining boundaries[73]. Assumed or subconscious, paradigms frame our thoughts, and enable us to see and understand. In this sense, paradigms are not the thoughts we have, but they are the mental tools or mindsets that we use to understand a situation.

Neurotheology places the paradigms of science, particularly those sciences involving the brain and mind, and religion in relation to each other which means a discipline within the system does not supersede the other. Instead, as in the case of neurotheology, each perspective maintains a particular paradigm to understand the relationship between the brain and mind: the metaphysical claims of both science and religion are recognized under the principle of personal ultimacy.

2) Typology

Neurotheology encompasses scientific and theological relationships involving numerous different and contradicting positions. Inevitably, varying scientific and theological positions need room provided by the other. Various scientific and religious positions decrease while the others increase, or in a sense religion "crosses" to science, and science "crosses" to religion. Both science and religion stand to sacrifice of their identities in order to relate, share meaningfully, and produce a relevant message. Typologies are important methodological instruments applied to relate often contradictory, opposing mind/body paradigms and achieve the abovementioned goal.

Typologies are frameworks that allow researchers to make meaning from the positions of dissonance and consonance within science and religion. A typology is a characterization or schema, an ordering or construction of the types of their relationships. Typologies disclose goals and aims for their interaction, and illuminate underlying assumptions shaping both public and private discussion[74]. Despite the limitations of any given scientific or religious perspective, a typology serves as a constructed series in which the various persuasions in both fields associate to emphasize their similar and dissimilar unity.

Ian Barbour's typology, the most widely applied in the field of neurotheology, covers the basic structural areas for relating science and religion. His typology includes four dimensions: conflict, independence, dialogue and integration. Each of these dimensions plays its own important role in neurotheological research:

- The concept of *conflict* signifies that science and religion stand as mutually exclusive perspectives which maintain two separate worlds. This is best exemplified by Biblical literalism and scientific materialism;
- *Independence* maintains that science and religion employ contrasting methods and communicate in different languages;
- Through *dialogue* the disciplines identify boundary questions from each and establish methodological parallels to initiate and maintain discussion;
- And finally, *integration* comprises positions that have systematically synthesized: for example, natural theology and theology of nature[75].

Thus, acknowledging the tensions between science and religion, the concept of sacrificial re-birth embraces the mind/body conflict thus making it possible for neurotheology to encompass scientific and theological positions of difference, similarity and contradiction.

3) Ritual Experience

Ritual experience serves as an instrument to synchronize and harmonize the opposites of human existence. D'Aquili and Newberg argue that we live between two "Ultimate poles of mythic structure"[76]: humanity and some form of superhuman power. Humans are compelled to make their existence by repeatedly relating these two opposites. The concept of ritual experience/habit suggests existence of certain rhyme, rhythm and reason in human living.

Human behavior within the realm of religion and life in general involves life-sustaining and life-shaping repetitive behavior. Ritual experience is our sure way to make life happen, whether experimenting using repetitive scientific methodology or leading religious lives, personal and communal. We need not devalue or forsake the meaning of ritual experience for us. As humans we will repeat our steps—in a manner of speaking and a matter of time. Neurotheology attempts to speak to the need for both science and theology to continually return to the rooms for discussion and re-appropriation. With every generation comes nuance for change. We repeat our journeys, re-state our arguments and measure the growth in our steps only to redraw the circumference of our life patterns larger. We are more indebted to geometric patterns of circles and ellipses, than straight lines and boxes.

4) Inner life

Each human being lives similarly complicated inner life filled with conflicts, intervals of peace and rest, memories and hopes which are expressed in thoughts and behaviors. Inner life speaks to inner space inhabited with perceptions of self, others, the world, and spiritual awareness. For some we are at play with multiple inside partners; orchestrating harmony is primary. For others we are at war; orchestrating triumph over self and evil forces is paramount. Neurotheology encompasses the complexity of inner human experience including the recognition that spiritual or nonmaterial forces are interplay within each and every human being.

The methodological concept of inner life asserts the root relationship existing between the spiritual, and the mental, and body or material realities of humanity: "Wherefore the spirit is for us not only the seat of religion but its nearest world. The universe portrays itself in the inner life, and then the corporeal is comprehensible from the spiritual"[77]. Through this concept, neurotheology acknowledges and accepts the influence of the spirit world in shaping who and what we are.

The concept of inner life addresses the complexity of human existence as conceived by science and religion, both internal and external, helping us perceive what we perceive regardless of the names we give to the perceived phenomena either within the scientific or religious paradigm.

CRITICISM

The key problem with neurotheology is the attempt to unify two strikingly different perspectives on human being within one discipline. The discrepancy between the theological and scientific perspectives has recently received much attention both domestically and internationally[78]. Yet, the origins of this discrepancy can be traced back to the emergency of modern science when Galileo, Descartes and Newton dramatically changed traditional patterns of perception of the world and man.

The so-called 'decade of the brain' marked by significant advances in research and mapping of human brain led to reinforcement of the neuroscientific perspective on human being. Underlying principles and ideas of neuroscience are much at variance with those shaping the traditional perspective on humans which has been dominant for centuries.

The neuroscientific perspective has grave implications on established views on the mental dimension of human being and seriously questions validity of such concepts as mind, selfhood, will, consciousness and freedom. Thus, neuroscience perspective denies the traditional perception of free will claiming it is "...based upon a serious misunderstanding, because our character, our sexual preference, our eventual criminality and all our other important characteristics are already determined on the level of the brain"[79]. Also, according to the neuroscientific approach, human consciousness as such is secondary with respect to brain processes: decisions human beings perceive as made by their consciousness are, in fact, made and determined by their brain processes[80].

The new approach to understanding and explaining mental dimension of human life brings neuroscience to a conflict with theology that has claimed mental domain since long ago. There are at least three major reasons for such conflict:

I.   Firstly, freedom, mind, responsibility, consciousness and other attributes belonging to the domain of spirituality have traditionally been recognized as ontologically fundamental characteristics of human;

2.   Secondly, empirical research methods have never been applied to study the spiritual phenomena. Consequently, spirituality has been referred to the special domain of theology;

3.   And thirdly, after Rene Descartes (1596-1650) provided a philosophical exposition of distinction between primary and secondary qualities thus establishing the dualistic model of the world (mental vs. material), the agency of God with respect to material substances had turned hardly possible to conceive. The same was valid in regard of the human mind's agency to the body. Consequently, the focus of theology shifted to spirituality, and by lapse of time this tendency only strengthened: "Since Descartes, and especially since Kant, this view that God can only be talked about in the domain of the human subject—of the human mind with its morality and freedom—has received ever more resonance in theology"[81].

As a result of the latter nature—representing the material world— has been fully neglected as a subject of theological discourses and reflections. This consequence is especially important for it questions the scientific value of neurotheology as such.

The long history of conflicting relations between science and spirituality is arguably the most important concern in regard to Neurotheology currently. Over centuries, theology has attempted everything possible to fight and smother advance of science that offers an opposite perspective on theological subjects. As western science developed, theologians passed over to the strategy of bypassing the traps revealed by science. The result of such relationship is the two strikingly different worldviews and lack of any empirical formulations that can serve as the cornerstone for a joint discipline.

The recent advances of neuroscience have contributed to making the problem of incompatibility between science and theology even more complex. Many studies establishing the dependence of spiritual domain on the brain imply that concepts and approaches developed within traditional theology have lost their validity. Apparently, theology must develop such approaches and insights that would provide entirely different vision of material nature.

Furthermore, some neuroscientists put in question the notion that freedom, mind, responsibility, consciousness and other attributes belonging to the domain of spirituality are ontologically fundamental characteristics of human. Thus, Patricia and Paul Churchland, Terry

Sejnowski and other scientists leaning to a more reductionist position demonstrate strong biological bias in their views on religious beliefs and spiritual experiences. Establishing the underlying material basis for these characteristics, representatives of this position seriously undermine positions of traditional theology. The basic question is whether such fundamentally different perspectives on spirituality and human being can coexist within one discipline? This question seems reasonable considering the fact that some existing disciplines (e.g. behavioral and social neuroscience, psychology) are equipped good enough to effectively study the realm of spirituality[82].

While the reductionist position is still vocal enough to generate the above criticism, the approach of Newberg, D'Aquili and their followers is moderate enough to avoid it. It offers additional ways to understand the development, endurance and reasons for religious beliefs without strong emphasis being put on antecedence of biology. Evidently, this position does not generate any conflict with freedom, mind, responsibility, and consciousness as ontologically fundamental characteristics of human.

Another portion of criticism concerns the notion of neurotheology as a collaborative multidisciplinary approach contributing to better understanding of each discipline encompassed by it. Some authors believe that even if neuroscience and theology are brought together within the discipline of neurotheology, the differences will inevitably lead to one discipline, namely theology, dominating the other.

Theology is an established discipline with well-developed philosophic theories and a number of dogmas, while neuroscience is a comparatively new field of knowledge about the physical world. When attempting to bring them under one perspective one must be extremely cautious to maintain balanced attitude toward both. Failure to do this results in unjustified use of any more or less appropriate and reliable scientific evidences as "...a full-fledged validation of some esoteric philosophy or system of faith"[83]. In other words, there is risk of a hidden agenda motivating the theologians to employ the scientific evidences, namely to provide scientific justification for obsolete and unjustifiable tenets of the faith.

CONCLUSION

Humans exist in the world encompassing three distinct dimensions: physical, mental and spiritual. Each of these dimensions exerts strong influence on our lives and experiences. Neurotheology emerges as a highly dynamic approach that attempts to establish a bridge between the scientific approaches and the world of human mind and spirituality represented by beliefs and belief systems. Neurotheology in the broader sense provides the much-needed place for the two historically incompatible approaches allowing them to make sense of their differences. Neurotheology connects the study and conceptualization of the human brain and the philosophical interpretations of mind to the variety of beliefs and belief systems developed by the human being.

Although our knowledge on the neural bases of spirituality and beliefs is far from being comprehensive, a number of studies have confirmed the notion of biological foundations underlying these phenomena. On the other hand, the methodological framework employed by neurotheology allows relating the neurological phenomena to spirituality and beliefs, in this case mystical and religious. The four methodological concepts of personal ultimacy, sacrificial re-birth, ritual experience, and inner life serve as an effective tool to connect science and religion in such a way to address the wide range of issues associated with the brain/mind relationship, internal and external religious responses, etc.

Neurotheology should not be perceived as an isolated discipline attempting to establish the missing link between the human being and God. The attempt to relate neuroscience and religion demonstrates how neurotheology can be applied to make good on the current claim of neuroscience in various fields providing the room to encompass the variety of beliefs and belief systems. Neurotheology affords different branches of scientific inquiry opportunity to develop distinct approaches to brain and mind representative of their own propensity. Within the focus of this paper neurotheology postulates that various scientific and religious systems can coexist within one discipline without one field of knowledge dominating the other, nor a particular persuasion or propensity within a field under another.

Thus, neurotheology as a collaborative approach between science and theology accomplishes the following tasks:

1. Facilitates meaningful dialogue across academic disciplines;
2. Elucidates the human condition by interpreting and explaining human thinking, feeling, behavior, and experience in light of brain, mind, and belief perspectives;
3. Creates and sustains academic vigor sufficient and varied for secondary, college and university training;
4. Offers both clinical and social applications, and pedagogical uses.

Being an attempt to marry a materialistic discipline of neuroscience to beliefs and spirituality, neurotheology attracts much criticism. In the case of science-religion relationship, the criticism is mainly philosophical dealing with the incompatibility between the diametrically opposite realms of science and spirituality. The notion of neurotheology as a collaborative multidisciplinary approach contributing to better understanding of each discipline encompassed by it is also criticized. Some authors believe that even if neuroscience and theology are brought together within the discipline of neurotheology, the differences will inevitably lead to one discipline, namely theology, dominating the other.

Despite validity, at least partial, of the criticism, neurotheology still remains the only contemporary perspective to provide a unified framework to study and relate the mental, physical and spiritual variances of human existence. With the right approach to limitations of neurotheology, this perspective may serve humankind well far into the future.

Notes

Endnotes

Introduction

[1] Lipton, B., *The Biology of Belief: Unleashing The Power of Consciousness, Matter and Miracles*, Mountain of Love, 2005.

[2] Hamer, D., *The God Gene*, Doubleday, 2004.

[3] Newberg, A. "Neurotheology." *BookRags*. Retrieved 23 June 2006, from the World Wide Web. http://www.bookrags.com/other/religion/neurotheology-eorl-10.html

[4] D'Aquili, E, and A. Newberg. *The Mystical Mind: Probing the Biology of Religious Experience, Theology and the Sciences*, Minneapolis, MN: Augsburg Fortress, 1999: 119.

[5] Huxley, A. *Island*, NY: Harper & Row, 1962: 172.

[6] Ashbrook, J. "Neurotheology: The Working Brain and the Work of Theology?" *Zygon*, 19, 3, 1984: 331-350.

[7] Fontana, D. *Psychology, religion, and spirituality*, Malden, MA: BPS Blackwell, 2003.

[8] McKinney, Laurence O. *Neurotheology: Virtual Religion in the 21st Century*. Cambridge, Massachusetts: American Institute for Mindfulness, 1994.

[9] Joseph, R. (ed.) *Neurotheology: Brain, Science, Spirituality, Religious Experience*. University Press, 2002

[10] Begley, S., and Underwood, A. "Religion and the brain". *Newsweek*, 137 (19), 2001: 50-58.

[11] Ibid, 53.

Main Discussion

[12] "Aquinas, Saint Thomas," Microsoft® Encarta® (http://encarta.msn.com On-line Encyclopaedia: Microsoft Corporation. 1997-2000.

[13] Frederick Copleston, in Chapter 37 to *A History of Philosophy*, Vol. 2, Double Day Press: New York, 1999: 376.

[14] Davidson, D. "Mental Events". In: D. Davidson, *Actions and Events,* Oxford: Clarendon, 1980.

[15] Szubka, T. and R. Warner, (Eds.), *Honderich: Articles on Functionalism, Identity Theories, the Union Theory, the Mind-Body Problem: The Current State of the Debate,* Blackwells, Oxford, 1994.

[16] Papineau, D. and H. Selina, *Introducing Consciousness,* Icon Books, 2000: 27.

[17] Ibid.

[18] Guinness, Alma E. ed., *ABC's of the Human Mind,* Pleasantville, New York: The Reader's Digest Association, 1990: 64.

[19] Ibid, 70-72.

[20] Persinger MA. "Religious and mystical experiences as artifacts of temporal lobe function: a general hypothesis". *Percept Mot Skills* 1983, 57: 1255-1262.

[21] Persinger MA. "Enhanced incidence of the "sensed presence" in people who have learned to meditate: support for the right hemispheric intrusion hypothesis". *Percept Mot Skills* 1992, 65: pp.1308-1310

[22] Guthrie, C., "Neurology, Ritual, and Religion: An Initial Exploration; Or: "Were you there when they stimulated our amygdalas? Sometimes it causes me to tremble." *Proceedings for the North American Academy of Liturgy*, 2000: pp.107-124. [Paper given to the Ritual-Language-Action Group, NAAL, Tampa, 2000.]

[23] Ibid.

[24] Ashbrook, J. B., and Albright, C. R., *The humanizing brain: Where religion and neuroscience meet,* Cleveland: The Pilgrim Press, 1997: 8.

[25] Ibid.

[26] Ibid, 10-11.

[27] Ibid.

[28] Ibid.

[29] Ibid, 16.

[30] Ibid.

[31] Ibid, 22.

[32] Rottschaefer, W. A., "The image of God of neurotheology: Reflections of culturally based religious commitments or evolutionarily based neuroscientific theories?" *Zygon*, 1999, 34: 60.

[33] Ashbrook, J. B., and Albright, C. R., *The humanizing brain: Where religion and neuroscience meet,* Cleveland: The Pilgrim Press, 1997.

[34] Ibid, 52.

[35] Ibid, 53-55.

[36] Ashbrook, J. B., and Albright, C. R., *The humanizing brain: Where religion and neuroscience meet,* Cleveland: The Pilgrim Press, 1997: 58.

[37] Ibid.

[38] Simmons, J.K., "Neurotheology and Spiritual Transformation: Clues in the Work of Joel Goldsmith", *Western Illinois University*. Retrieved 23 June 2006, from the World Wide Web. www.wiu.edu/users/mfjks/ntgs.html.doc

[39] Newberg, A., and E. D'Aquili, *Why God Won't Go Away*, NY: Ballatine Books, 2001: 50-51.

[40] D'Aquili, E, and A. Newberg. *The Mystical Mind: Probing the Biology of Religious Experience, Theology and the Sciences*, Minneapolis, MN: Augsburg Fortress, 1999: 55

[41] Ibid.

[42] Ibid.

[43] Simmons, J.K., "Neurotheology and Spiritual Transformation: Clues in the Work of Joel Goldsmith", *Western Illinois University*. Retrieved 23 June 2006, from the World Wide Web. www.wiu.edu/users/mfjks/ntgs.html.doc

[44] Rottschaefer, W. A., "The image of God of neurotheology: Reflections of culturally based religious commitments or evolutionarily based neuroscientific theories?" *Zygon*, 1999, 34: 59.

[45] Ashbrook, J. B., and Albright, C. R., *The humanizing brain: Where religion and neuroscience meet*, Cleveland: The Pilgrim Press, 1997: 39.

[46] Simmons, J.K., "Neurotheology and Spiritual Transformation: Clues in the Work of Joel Goldsmith", *Western Illinois University*. Retrieved 23 June 2006, from the World Wide Web. www.wiu.edu/users/mfjks/ntgs.html.doc

[47] Newberg, A., and E. D'Aquili, *Why God Won't Go Away*, NY: Ballatine Books, 2001: 33.

[48] D'Aquili, E, and A. Newberg. *The Mystical Mind: Probing the Biology of Religious Experience, Theology and the Sciences*, Minneapolis, MN: Augsburg Fortress, 1999: 22.

[49] Ibid.

[50] Ibid, 22.

[51] Ibid, 22.

[52] Ibid, 22-23.

[53] Van Gelder, T.J., "Monism, Dualism, Pluralism" *Mind and Language*, Vol.13, 1998: pp.76-97.

[54] Fedorko, L (Ed.) (1986), *Understanding Psychology*, New York: Random House

[55] Maddi, S. R. *Personality theories: A comparative analysis* (6th ed.). Toronto: Brooks/Cole Publishing Co., 1966.

[56] Bruner, J. "Culture and human development: A new look". *Human development*, 33, 1990: 344.

[57] Gleitman, H., A. Friedlund, and Reisberg, D., *Basic Psychology*, W.W. Norton and Co., 2000: 140.

[58] Vander Zanden, J. W. and W. James, *Human development* (5th edition), McGraw-Hill Inc., 1993.

[59] Skinner, B., "Reply to Harnad's article, "What are the scope and limits of radical behaviorist theory?" *Behavioral and Brain Sciences*, 7, 1984: pp.721-724.

[60] Ormrod, J., *Educational Psychology: Principles and applications*, Prentice-Hall, 1995.

[61] Vander Zanden, J. W. and W. James, *Human development* (5th edition), McGraw-Hill Inc., 1993.

[62] Lewin, K., *Field Theory in Social Science*, Tavistock, London, 1952: 288

[63] Pinel, J.P.J., *Biopsychology* (4th ed.). Boston: Allyn and Bacon, 2000.

[64] MacLennan, B., "Evolutionary Neurotheology and the Varieties of Religious Experience."In Joseph, R. (Ed). *Neurotheology: Brain, Science, Spirituality, Religious Experience*, University Press, California, 2002: 305-315.

What is Neurotheology

[65] Copenhagen, R., "Thomas Reid's Philosophy of Mind: Consciousness and Intentionality", *Philosophy Compass*, Vol. 1, 3, 2006: 279.

[66] Anderson, R. S. *The Shape of Practical Theology: Empowering Ministry with Theological Praxis*, Downers Grove: Intervarsity Press, 2001: 24.

[67] Schleiermacher, F., "Second Speech" to *On Religion: Speeches to Its Cultured Despisers*, (trans. John Oman Louisville), Kentucky: Westminster/John Knox Press, 1994: 45-46.

[68] Schleiermacher, F., *On Religion: Speeches to Its Cultured Despisers.* New York: Harper & Brothers, Publishers, 1958 edition: 27.

[69] Gerrish, B. A. "Schleiermacher, Friedrich Daniel Ernst," from *The Oxford Companion to Christian Thought*, Hastings, A. Mason, and H. Pyper (eds.), Oxford: Oxford University Press, 2000: 644.

[70] Kreeft, P., and R. K. Tacelli, "Metaphysics". In: *Catholic Encyclopedia Handbook of Christian Apologetics*. Retrieved 23 June 2006, from the World Wide Web. http://www.newadvent.org/cathen/b.htm

[71] Ibid.

[72] Ibid.

[73] Ibid.

[74] Southgate, Ch. et al., (eds.), *God, Humanity and the Cosmos,* Harrisburg, Pennsylvania: Trinity Press International, 1999: 9-14.

[75] Ibid.

[76] D'Aquili, E, and A. Newberg. *The Mystical Mind: Probing the Biology of Religious Experience, Theology and the Sciences*, Minneapolis, MN: Augsburg Fortress, 1999: 88.

[77] Schleiermacher, F., "Second Speech" to *On Religion: Speeches to Its Cultured Despisers*, (trans. John Oman Louisville), Kentucky: Westminster/John Knox Press, 1994: 71.

Criticism

[78] Brown, W.S., N. Murphy, and H. N. Malony (Eds.), *Whatever Happened to the Soul? Scientific and Theological Portraits of Human Nature*, Minneapolis, MA: Fortress Press, 1998.

[79] Oomen, P., "Towards a Neurotheology of the Person", *Grant Application for a Postdoctoral Project*, 'Innovatiefonds' University of Nijmegen, 2001. Retrieved 23 June 2006, from the World Wide Web. http://oase.uci.ru.nl/~arnow/neurotheology.pdf

[80] Ibid.

[81] Ibid.

[82] Ovalekar, M.N., ""Neurotheology": A semantic trap set by pseudo-science for the unwary scientist", *Centre for Neuroscientific Studies*, 2006. Retrieved 23 June 2006, from the World Wide Web. http://www.cns.res.in/neurotheology.html

[83] Ibid.

REFERENCES

Anderson, R. S. *The Shape of Practical Theology: Empowering Ministry with Theological Praxis*, Downers Grove: Intervarsity Press, 2001

Ashbrook, James "Neurotheology: The Working Brain and the Work of Theology?" *Zygon*, 19, 3, 1984: pp.331-350

Ashbrook, J. B., and Albright, C. R. *The humanizing brain: Where religion and neuroscience meet,* Cleveland: The Pilgrim Press, 1997

Begley, S., and Underwood, A. "Religion and the brain". *Newsweek*, 137 (19), 2001: pp.50-58

Brown, W.S., N. Murphy, and H. N. Malony (Eds.), *Whatever Happened to the Soul? Scientific and Theological Portraits of Human Nature*, Minneapolis, MA: Fortress Press, 1998

Bruner, J. "Culture and human development: A new look". *Human development*, 33, 1990: pp. 344-355.

Copenhagen, R., "Thomas Reid's Philosophy of Mind: Consciousness and Intentionality", *Philosophy Compass*, Vol. 1, 3, 2006: p.279

D'Aquili, E., and A. Newberg. *The Mystical Mind: Probing the Biology of Religious Experience,* Theology and the Sciences, Minneapolis, MN: Augsburg Fortress, 1999

Davidson, D. "Mental Events". In: D. Davidson, *Actions and Events,* Oxford: Clarendon, 1980

Fedorko, L (Ed.) (1986), *Understanding Psychology*, New York: Random House

Fontana, D. *Psychology, religion, and spirituality*, Malden, MA: BPS Blackwell, 2003

Gerrish, B. A. "Schleiermacher, Friedrich Daniel Ernst," from *The Oxford Companion to Christian Thought,* Hastings, A. Mason, and H. Pyper (eds.), Oxford: Oxford University Press, 2000: pp.644-646.

Gleitman, H., A. Friedlund, and Reisberg, D., *Basic Psychology*, W.W. Norton and Co., 2000

Guinness, Alma E. ed., *ABC's of the Human Mind,* Pleasantville, New York: The Reader's Digest Association, 1990.

Guthrie, C., "Neurology, Ritual, and Religion: An Initial Exploration; Or: "Were you there when they stimulated our amygdalas? Sometimes it causes me to tremble." *Proceedings for the North American Academy of Liturgy*, 2000: pp.107-124. [Paper given to the Ritual-Language-Action Group, NAAL, Tampa, 2000.]

Hamer, D., *The God Gene*, Doubleday, 2004

Joseph, R. (ed.) *Neurotheology: Brain, Science, Spirituality, Religious Experience.* University Press, 2002

Kreeft, P., and R. K. Tacelli, "Metaphysics". In: *Catholic Encyclopedia Handbook of Christian Apologetics.* Retrieved 23 June 2006, from the World Wide Web. http://www.newadvent.org/cathen/b.htm

Lipton, B., *The Biology Of Belief: Unleashing The Power Of Consciousness, Matter And Miracles*, Mountain of Love, 2005

Lewin, K., *Field Theory in Social Science*, Tavistock, London, 1952

MacLennan, B., "Evolutionary Neurotheology and the Varieties of Religious Experience". In Joseph, R. (Ed). *Neurotheology: Brain, Science, Spirituality, Religious Experience*, University Press, California, 2002

Maddi, S. R. *Personality theories: A comparative analysis* (6th ed.). Toronto: Brooks/Cole Publishing Co., 1966

McKinney, Laurence O. *Neurotheology: Virtual Religion in the 21st Century.* Cambridge, Massachusetts: American Institute for Mindfulness, 1994.

Newberg, Andrew. "Neurotheology." *BookRags.* Retrieved 23 June 2006, from the World Wide Web. http://www.bookrags.com/other/religion/neurotheology-eorl-10.html

Newberg, A., and E. D'Aquili, *Why God Won't Go Away*, NY: Ballatine Books, 2001

Oomen, P., "Towards a Neurotheology of the Person", *Grant Application for a Postdoc Project*, 'Innovatiefonds' University of Nijmegen, 2001. Retrieved 23 June 2006, from the World Wide Web. http://oase.uci.ru.nl/~arnow/neurotheology.pdf.

Ormrod, J., *Educational Psychology: Principles and applications*, Prentice-Hall, 1995

Ovalekar, M.N., ""Neurotheology": A semantic trap set by pseudo-science for the unwary scientist", *Centre for Neuroscientific Studies*, 2006. Retrieved 23 June 2006, from the World Wide Web. http://www.cns.res.in/neurotheology.html

Papineau, D. and H. Selina, *Introducing Consciousness*, Icon Books, 2000

Persinger MA. "Religious and mystical experiences as artifacts of temporal lobe function: a general hypothesis". *Percept Mot Skills* 1983, 57: pp.1255-1262.

Persinger MA. "Enhanced incidence of the "sensed presence" in people who have learned to meditate: support for the right hemispheric intrusion hypothesis". *Percept Mot Skills* 1992, 65: pp.1308-1310

Pinel, J.P.J., *Biopsychology* (4th ed.). Boston: Allyn and Bacon, 2000

Rottschaefer, W. A., "The image of God of neurotheology: Reflections of culturally based religious commitments or evolutionarily based neuroscientific theories?" *Zygon*, 1999, 34: pp.57-65.

Schleiermacher, F., *On Religion: Speeches to Its Cultured Despisers.* New York: Harper & Brothers, Publishers, 1958 edition

Schleiermacher, F., "Second Speech" to *On Religion: Speeches to Its Cultured Despisers*, (trans. John Oman Louisville), Kentucky: Westminster/John Knox Press, 1994

Szubka, T. and R. Warner, (Eds.), *Honderich: Articles on Functionalism, Identity Theories, the Union Theory, the Mind-Body Problem: The Current State of the Debate,* Blackwell, Oxford, 1994

Skinner, B., "Reply to Harnad's article, "What are the scope and limits of radical behaviorist theory?" *Behavioral and Brain Sciences*, 7, 1984: pp.721-724.

Simmons, J.K., "Neurotheology and Spiritual Transformation: Clues in the Work of Joel Goldsmith", *Western Illinois University*. Retrieved 23 June 2006, from the World Wide Web. www.wiu.edu/users/mfjks/ntgs.html.doc

Southgate, Ch. et al., (eds.), *God, Humanity and the Cosmos,* Harrisburg, Pennsylvania: Trinity Press International, 1999.

Van Gelder, T.J., "Monism, Dualism, Pluralism" *Mind and Language*, Vol.13, 1998: pp.76-97

Vander Zanden, J. W. and W. James, *Human development* (5th edition), McGraw-Hill Inc., 1993

Sources

Ackerman, S. (2006). *Hard Science, Hard Choices: Facts, Ethics, and Policies Guiding Brain Science Today.* Washington DC: Dana Press.

Alberts, B. (1997). *Science and Creationism: A View from the National Academy of Sciences* (2nd ed.). Washington, DC: National Academies Press.

Albright, C. & Ashbrook, J. (2001). *Where God Lives in the Human Brain* (2nd ed.). Naperville, IL: Sourcebooks Inc.

Alper, M. (2000). *The "God" Part of the Brain: A Scientific Interpretation of Human Spirituality and God* (5th ed.). New York: Rogue Press.

Alston, W. P. (1991). The Experiential Basis of Theism. *In The Telling the Truth Telling Project, Leadership University.* Retrieved April 9, 2007 from http://www.leaderu.com/truth/3truth04.html.

_____. (2003). What Is Naturalism, that We Should Be Mindful of It? *In The Telling the Truth Telling Project, Leadership University.* Retrieved April 9, 2007 from
http://www.leaderu.com/aip/docs/alston-naturalism.html.

Andresen, J. (Ed.). (2005). *Religion in Mind: Cognitive Perspectives on Religious Beliefs, Ritual and Experience.* New York, NY: Cambridge University Press.

_____. & Forman, R.K.C. (Eds.). (2000). *Cognitive Models and Spiritual Maps: Interdisciplinary Exploration of Religious Experience (Journal of Consciousness Studies)* Charlottesville, VA: Imprint Academic.

The Antimoderns: Six Postmodern Christians Discuss the Possibilities and Limits of Postmodernism. (2000, November 13). *Christianity Today Magazine Vol. 44*, No. 13, p. 74. See also, www.ChristianityToday.com.

Aquinas, Saint Thomas. (2007). In *Microsoft Encarta.* Retrieved April 9, 2007 Microsoft Encarta: http://encarta.msn.com/encyclopedia_761577720/Aquinas_Saint_Thomas.html.

Ashbrook, J. B. (1986). Brain, Mind and God. *The Christian Century, March 19-26, p. 295.* Retrieved April, 9, 2007 from http://www.religion-online.org/showarticle.asp?title=1027.

_____. (1990) *Faith and Ministry in Light of the Double Brain.* Lima, OH: Wyndham Hall Press.

_____., & Albright, C. R. (1997). *The Humanizing Brain: Where Religion and Neuroscience Meet.* Cleveland, OH: The Pilgrim Press.

Atomism. (2007). In *Encyclopedia Britannica Online.* Retrieved April 9, 2007, from Encyclopedia Britannica Online: http://www.britannica.com/ebc/article-9356082.

Austin, J.H. (1999). *Zen and the Brain: Towards An Understanding of Meditation and Consciousness.* Cambridge, Massachusetts: The MIT Press.

Baars, B. J. (2001). *In the Theater of Consciousness: The Workspace of the Mind* New York, NY: Oxford University Press USA.

Barber, E. W., & Barber, P. T. (2004). *When They Severed Earth from Sky: How the Human Mind Shapes Myth.* Princeton, NJ: Princeton University Press.

Barbour, I. G. (1997). *Religion and Science: Historical and Contemporary Issues.* New York, NY: HarperCollins Publishers, Inc.

_____. (2000). *When Science Meets Religion: Enemies, Strangers, or Partners?* New York, NY: HarperCollins Publishers.

Barrett, J. L. (2004). *Why Would Anyone Believe in God?* Lanham, MD: Alta Mira Press.

Bar-Yam, Y. (2000). Reductionism. In Concepts in Complex Systems. Retrieved April 9, 2007 from http://necsi.org/guide/concepts/reductionism.html, see also http://necsi.org/faculty/bar-yam.html.

Batson, D. C., Schoenrade, P., Ventis, L. W. (1993). *Religion and the Individual: A Social-Psychological Perspective.* New York, NY: Oxford University Press USA.

Baum, E. B. (2004). *What is thought?* Cambridge, MA: The MIT Press.

Baumann, G. (1999). *The Multicultural Riddle: Rethinking National, Ethnic, and Religious Identities (Zones of Religion)* New York, NY: Routledge-Taylor & Francis Group.

Baumer, F. (1978). *Main Currents of Western Thought: Readings in Western Europe Intellectual History from the Middle Ages to the Present, Fourth Edition.* New Haven, CT: Yale University Press.

Beit-Hallahmi, B., & Argyle, M. (1997). *The Psychology of Religious Behaviors, Belief & Experience.* New York: Routledge-Taylor & Francis Group.

Beloff, J. (1994). Dualism: The Mind-Brain Problem. Retrieved April 9, 2007 from http://moebius.psy.ed.ac.uk/-dualism/papers/brains. html. Originally published in *The Journal of Scientific Exploration*, *Vol. 8*, Number 4.

Bennett, M. R. & Hacker, P.M.S. (2003). *Philosophical Foundations of Neuroscience* Malden, MA: Blackwell Publishing Limited.

The Bible: King James Version. (1996). Atlanta, GA: Thomas Nelson Publishers.

Big Bang Theory. (2007). In *Encyclopedia Britannica Online*. Retrieved April 9, 2007 from Encyclopedia Britannica Online: http://www.britannica.com/ebc/article-9357237.

Bloom, H. (2001). *Global Brain: The Evolution of Mass Mind from the Big Bang to the 21st Century*. Hoboken, NJ: Wiley.

Bohlin, R. (1993). The Five Crises in Evolutionary Theory. *Probe Ministries*. Retrieved April 9, 2007 from http://www.probe.org/content/view/6/67/.

_____. (1996). Evolution's Big Bang. *Probe Ministries*. Retrieved April 9, 2007 from http://www.probe.org/content/view/51/67/.

_____., & Bohlin, S. (1993). How to Talk to Your Kids About Evolution and Creation. *Probe Ministries*. Retrieved April 9, 2007 from http://www.leaderu.com/orgs/probe/docs/cr-evol.html.

Bohlin, S. (1999). Evidence for God's Existence. *Probe Ministries*. Retrieved April 9, 2007 from http://www.probe.org/content/view/638/0/.

Bower, B. (2000, September 30). Memory Echoes in Brain's Sensory Terrain. *Science News Online, Vol. 158*, No. 14, p. 213. Retrieved April 9, 2007 from http://www.sciencenews.org/articles/20000930/fob3.asp.

Boyer, P. (1994). *The Naturalness of Religious Ideas: A Cognitive Theory of Religion*. Berkeley: University of California Press.

_____. (2002). *Religion Explained: The Evolutionary Origins of Religious Thought*. New York, NY: Basic Books.

Braidot, N. P. (2005). *Neuromarketing*. Madrid, Spain: Puertonorte-Sur.

Bransford, J. D., Brown, A. L., & Cocking, R. R., (Eds.). (1999). Mind and Brain, Chapter 5. In *How People Learn: Brain, Mind, Experience, and School, & How People Learn: Brain, Mind, Experience, and School Part II: Learners and Learning Committee on Developments in the Science of Learning*. (p.102-116). Commission on Behavioral and Social Sciences and Education. See also, http://books.nap.edu/openbook.php?record_id=6160&page=102. Washington, DC: National Academies Press.

Broom, D. M. (2003). *The Evolution of Morality and Religion.* New York, NY: Cambridge University Press.

Brothers, L. (1997). *Fridays Footprint: How Society Shapes the Human Mind.* New York, NY: Oxford University Press USA.

Brown, C. E. (2001). Pentecostalism. At the *Religious Movements Home Page Project.* Retrieved April 9, 2007 from The Religious Movements Home Page Project at the University of Virginia: http://religiousmovements.lib.virginia.edu/nrms/penta.html.

Buller, D. J. (2005). *Adapting Minds: Evolutionary Psychology and the Persistent Quest for Human Nature.* Cambridge, MA: The MIT Press.

Burke Jr., T. J. (1999). Preserving Theology and Science through Philosophy. *In The Telling the Truth Telling Project, Leadership University.* Retrieved April 9, 2007 from http://www.leaderu.com/offices/koons/docs/burke_t.html.

Burri, J. (2000). The Moral Consequences of the Big Bang Philosophy. Retrieved April 9, 2007 from http://www.bigbang.org/comple-e.htm.

Bynum, E. B. (1999). *The African Unconsciousness: Roots of Ancient Mysticism and Modern Psychology.* New York, NY: Teachers College Press.

Calvin, W. H. (1996). *How Brains Think: Evolving Intelligence, Then and Now.*New York, NY: Basic Books.

_____. (1998). *The Cerebral Code: Thinking a Thought in the Mosaics of the Mind.* Cambridge, MA: The MIT Press.

Camerer, C. F. (2003). *Behavioral Game Theory: Experiments in Strategic Interaction (The Roundtable Series in Behavioral Economics).* Princeton, NJ: Princeton University Press.

Cardena, E., Lynn, S. J., Krippner, S. C. (Eds.). (2000). *Varieties of Anomalous Experience: Examining the Scientific Evidence.* Washington DC: American Psychological Association.

Carruthers, P., Stich, S., & Segal, M. (Eds.). (2002). *The Cognitive Basis of Science.* New York, NY: Cambridge University Press.

Cayuela, O. M., Requena, R. A., Romano, S. E., & Scinica, E. B. (2005). *Neuromarketing: Para Recrear la Confianza con los Clientes.* Buenos Aires, Argentina: Altagerencia.

Chakrabarti, K. K. (1999). *Classical Indian Philosophy of Mind: The Nyaya Dualist Tradition.* Albany, NY: State University of New York Press.

Churchland, P. (2002). *Brain-Wise: Studies in Neurophilosophy.* Cambridge, MA: The MIT Press.

Clark, A. (2000). *Mindware: An Introduction to the Philosophy of Cognitive Science.* New York, NY: Oxford University Press USA.

Clayton, P. (2006). *God and Contemporary Science, (Edinburgh studies in Constructive Theology, no. 9).* Grand Rapids, MI: Wm B. Eerdmans Publishing Company.

Cohen, S. (1988). *The Chemical Brain: The Neurochemistry of Addictive Disorders.* Minneapolis, MN: CompCare Publishers.

Coltheart, M., & Davies, M. (Eds.). (2000). *Pathologies of Belief (Readings in Mind and Language).* Malden, MA: Blackwell Publishing, Inc.

Connolly, W. E. (2002). *Neuropolitics: Thinking, Culture, Speed (Theory Out of Bounds, Number 23).* Minneapolis, MN: University of Minnesota Press.

Connor, S. (1997, October 29). The 'God spot' is found in Brain. *The Los Angeles Times.*

Copleston, F. (1994). *A History of Philosophy, vol. 2.* (reprint of 1950 ed.). New York, NY: Hyperion Books.

Cory Jr., G. A. (2003). *The Consilient Brain: The Bioneurological Basis of Economics, Society, and Politics.* (2nd. ed.). New York, NY: Springer Publishing.

Cox, H. (2001). *Fire From Heaven: The Rise of Pentecostal Spirituality and the Reshaping of Religion in the 21st Century.* Cambridge, MA: Da Capo Press.

Coyle, D. (2007). *The Soulful Science: What Economists Really Do and Why It Matters.* Princeton, NJ: Princeton University Press.

Creation Science Home Page. (http://emporium.turnpike.net/c/cs/)

Custance, A. (1977). Science and Faith. In The Door Way Papers Series, Vol. 8. (2001 ed.) Retrieved, April 9, 2007 from the Arthur Custance On-line Library: http://www.custance.org/Library/Volume8/index.html#About_the_Book

Dalai Lama. (1999). *Consciousness at the Crossroads: Conversations with the Dalai Lama on Brain Science and Buddhism.* Ithaca NY: Snow Lion Publications.

Dalton, C. W. (1990). *The Right Brian and Religion: A Discussion of Religion in the Context of the Right and Left Brain Theory.* Lakeside, CA: Big Blue Books.

D'Aquili, E., & Newberg, A. (1999). *The Mystical Mind: Probing the Biology of Religious Experience, Theology and the Sciences.* Minneapolis, MN: Augsburg Fortress Publishers.

Davidson, D. (2001). Anomalous Monism. In *MITECS: MIT Encyclopedia of Cognitive Sciences.* Retrieved April 9, 2007 from the MIT Encyclopedia of Cognitive Sciences: http://cognet. mit.edu/library/erefs/mitecs/.

Davies, P. (1993). *Mind of God: The Scientific Basis of a Rational World.* New York, NY: Simon & Schuster.

Deism. (2007). In *New Advent Catholic Encyclopedia.* Retrieved April 9, 2007 from The New Advent Catholic Encyclopedia: http:// www.newadvent.org/cathen/04679b.htm.

De Mey, Marc. (1992). *The Cognitive Paradigm.* Chicago, IL: University Of Chicago Press.

Dembski, W. A. (1994). The Fallacy of Contextualism. In *The Princeton Theological Review.* Reprinted in the Access Research Network on the World Wide Web: http://www.arn.org/docs/dembski/ wd_contexism.htm.

_____. (1996). Converting Matter into Mind. *In The Telling the Truth Telling Project, Leadership University.* Retrieved April 9, 2007 from http://www.leaderu.com/offices/dembski/docs/bd-converting.html.

_____. (1996). What Every Theologian should know about Creation, Evolution and Design. *In The Telling the Truth Telling Project, Leadership University.* Retrieved April 9, 2007 from http://www.leaderu.com/offices/dembski/docs/bd-theologn. html.

_____. (1998). Science and Design First Things. *In The Telling the Truth Telling Project, Leadership University.* Retrieved April 9, 2007 from http://www.facultylinc.com/personal/facoffice.nsf/ AllStaffbyStaffID/wdembskiOpenDocument.

Development of Atomic Theory. (2007). In *Encyclopedia Britannica Online.* Retrieved April 9, 2007 from Encyclopedia Britannica Online:

http://www.britannica.com/eb/article-9094956/atomic-theory.

Donahue III, M. J. (1997). An Introduction to Mathematical Chaos Theory and Fractal Geometry. Retrieved April 9, 2007 from *Fractal Finance,* http://www.fractalfinance.com/chaostheory. html.

Donald, M. (2002). *A Mind So Rare: The Evolution of Human Consciousness.* New York: NY: W. W. Norton & Company.

_____. (2005). *Origins of the Modern Mind: Three Stages in the Evolution of Culture and Cognition.* Cambridge, MA: Harvard University Press.

Drees, W. B. (1991). *Beyond the Big Bang: Quantum Cosmologies and God.* LaSalle, Illinois: Open Court publishing Company.

Dunne, B. J., & Jahn, R. G. (1987). *Margins Of Reality: The Role of Consciousness in the Physical World* , Orlando, FL: Harcourt Inc.

Eliade, M. (1981). *History of Religious Ideas, Volume 1: From the Stone Age to the Eleusinian Mysteries (History of Religious Ideas).* (W. R. Trask, Trans.). Chicago, IL: University of Chicago Press.

_____. (1988). *History of Religious Ideas: From Muhammad to the Age of Reforms (History of Religious Ideas) Vol.3* (A. Hiltebeitel & D. Apostolos-Cappadona, Trans.). Chicago, IL: University of Chicago Press.

Eliasmith, C. (2004). Epiphenomenalism. *Dictionary of Philosophy of Mind.* Retrieved April 9, 2007 from The Dictionary of Philosophy of Mind: http://philosophy.uwaterloo.ca/MindDict/epiphenomenalism.html.

_____., & Mandik, P. (2004). Functionalism. *Dictionary of Philosophy of Mind.* Retrieved April 9, 2007 from The Dictionary of Philosophy of Mind: http://philosophy.uwaterloo.ca/MindDict/functionalism.html.

Evans, D. (2001). *Emotion: The Science of Sentiment.* New York, NY: Oxford University Press USA.

Fackerell, M. (2007). Spiritual Warfare. ChristianFaith.com. *Retrieved* from http://www.christian-faith.com/forjesus/spiritual-warfare-breaking-curses.

Fauconnier, G., & Turner, M. (2002). *The Way We Think: Conceptual Blending and the Mind's Hidden Complexities.* New York, NY: Basic Books-The Perseus Books Group.

Fine, C. (2006). *A Mind of Its Own: How Your Brain Distorts and Deceives.* New York, NY: W. W. Norton.

Fowler, J. W. (1995). *Stages of Faith: The Psychology of Human Development and the Quest for Meaning.* New York: HarperCollins.

Frank, J. D., (1964). *Persuasion and Healing.* New York, NY: Schocken Publishing-Random House Publishing.

Francis, L. J. (2005). *Faith and Psychology: Personality, Religion and the Individual.* Nashville, TN: Abingdon Press.

Freeman, W. J. (2001). *How Brains Make Up Their Minds New York*, NY: Columbia University Press.

Frijda, N. H., Manstead, A., & Bem, S. (Eds.). (2006). *Emotions and Beliefs: How Feelings Influence Thoughts (Studies in Emotion and Social Interaction).* New York, NY: Cambridge University Press.

Fuller, A. R. (1994). *Psychology & Religion: Eight Points of View.* (3rd ed). Lanham, MD: Rowman & Littlefield Publishers, Inc.

Gardner, H. (2004). *Changing Minds: The Art and Science of Changing Our Own and Other People's Minds*. Cambridge, MA: Harvard Business School Press.

Gazzaniga, M. S. (Ed.). (1999). *The New Cognitive Neurosciences: Second Edition* Cambridge, MA: The MIT Press.

_____. (2005). *The Ethical Brain*. Washington, DC: Dana Press.

Gill, P. L. & Bohnert, D. A Realistic Definition of Determinism. The Cambridge Psychotherapy Institute Glossary- The Society Of Natural Science. Retrieved April 9, 2007 from http://www.determinism.com.

_____., & Bohnert, D. Determinism. The Cambridge Psychotherapy Institute Glossary- The Society Of Natural Science. Retrieved April 9, 2007 from http://www.determinism.com.

Gingerich, O. (1994). The Real Issue Is There a Role for Natural Theology Today? In M. Rae, H. Regan, & J. Stenhouse, (Eds.), Science *and Theology: Questions at the Interface* (p. 29-48). Edinburgh: T & T Clarke.

Giovannoli, J. & Wilson, D.A. (2001). *The Biology of Belief: How Our Biology Biases Our Beliefs and Perceptions*. info@rosettapress.com: Rosetta Press.

Glannon, W. (2007). *Defining Right and Wrong in Brain Science: Essential Readings in Neuroethics*. Washington DC: Dana Press.

Glimcher, P.W. (2004). *Decisions, Uncertainty, and the Brain: The Science of Neuroeconomics*. Cambridge, MA: The MIT Press.

Goertzel, T. (1992) *Turncoats & True Believers: The Dynamics of Political Belief and Disillusionment*. Amherst, NY: Prometheus Books.

Gould, S. J. (2002). *Rocks of Ages: Science and Religion in the Fullness of Life* (reprint ed.). New York, NY: Ballantine Books-Random House Publishing.

Graham, G. (2000). Behaviorism (revised 2005). *Stanford Encyclopedia of Philosophy*. Retrieved April 9, 2007 from The Stanford Encyclopedia of Philosophy: http://plato.stanford.edu/entries/behaviorism/.

Gregory, R. L. (Ed.). (2004). *The Oxford Companion to the Mind*. New York, NY: Oxford University Press USA.

Guinness, A. E., & Editors of Readers Digest. (1990). *ABC's of the Human Mind*. Pleasantville, NY: The Reader's Digest Association.

Guthrie, C. (2000). Neurology, Ritual, and Religion: An Initial Exploration; Or: 'Were you there when they stimulated our amygdalas? Sometimes it causes me to tremble *Proceedings for the North American Academy of Liturgy, 2000,* 107-124

Halsall, P. (1998). Thomas Paine: Of the Religion of Deism Compared with the Christian Religion. *The Modern History Sourcebook.* Retrieved April 9, 2007 from http://www.fordham.edu/halsall/mod/paine-deism.html.

Hamer, D. (2005). *The God Gene: How Faith is Hardwired into Our Genes.* New York, NY: Anchor Books.

Harnish, R. (2001). *Minds, Brains, Computers: An Historical Introduction to the Foundations of Cognitive Science.* Malden, MA: Blackwell Publishing Inc.

Harre, R. (2002). *Cognitive Science: A Philosophical Introduction* Thousand Oaks, CA: Sage Publications Ltd.

Hazen, Craig J. Philosophia Christiphilosophia Christi Journal of the Evangelical Philosophical Society: Philosophia Christi Biola University. E-mail: craig.hazen@biola.net La Mirada, CA Volume 21:1 1998.

Hefner, P. (1996). Science and Religion and the Search for Meaning. *Zygon: Journal of Religion and Science, Vol. 31* (2), 307–321

Helminiak, D. A. (1996). *The Human Core of Spirituality: Mind As Psyche and Spirit.* Albany, NY: State University of New York Press.

Hilliard III, A. G. (1998). *The Reawakening of the African Mind* (revised ed.). Gainesville, FL: Makare Publishing.

Honderich, T. (1994). Articles on Functionalism, Identity Theories, the Union Theory. In Szubka, T., & Warner, R. (Eds.), *The Mind-Body Problem: The Current State of the Debate.* Oxford: Blackwell Publishing.

Hooker, R. (2000). English Deism. *Internet Encyclopedia of Philosophy.* Retrieved April 9, 2007 from the Internet Encyclopedia of Philosophy:

http://www.sullivan-county.com/nfo/nov_2000/eng_deism.htm.

Horton, R. (1997). *Patterns of Thought in Africa and the West: Essays on Magic, Religion and Science.* New York, NY: Cambridge University Press.

Huntington, S., & Franklin, S. (1996). Process Thought from an Evangelical Perspective: An Appreciation and Critique. *Evangelical Perspective, Vol. 20*(1). See also, Center for Process Studies: http://www.ctr4process.org/.

Illes, J. (Ed.). (2005). *Neuroethics: Defining the Issues in Theory, Practice and Policy.* New York, NY: Oxford University Press USA.

Jacobs, L. (1992). *Religion and the Individual: A Jewish Perspective (Cambridge Studies in Religious Traditions).* New York, NY: Cambridge University Press.

James, W. (1994). *The Varieties of Religious Experience.* New York, NY: Modern Library-Random House Publishing. (first published 1902).

Jaynes, J. (1990). *The Origin of Consciousness in the Breakdown of the Bicameral Mind* (first published 1982). Boston, MA: Houghton Mifflin Company.

Jeeves, M. (1994). *Mind Fields: Reflections on the Science of Mind and Brain.* Grand Rapids, MI: Baker Books.

Johnson, M. (1994). *Moral Imagination: Implications of Cognitive Science for Ethics.* Chicago, IL: University of Chicago Press.

Johnson, P. E. (1992). What is Darwinism? Retrieved April 9, 2007 The Access Research Network: http://www.arn.org/docs/johnson/wid.htm.

Joseph, R., Newberg, A., Albright, C.R., James, W., Nietzsche, F., & Persinger, M. (2003). *Neurotheology: Brain, Science, Spirituality, Religious Experience* (2nd ed.). Lanham, MD: University Press.

Justice, B. (2000). *Who Gets Sick: How Beliefs, Moods and Thoughts Affect Health* (revised ed.). Derbyshire, UK: Peak Press

Keas, M. (1988). Thomas Aquinas and the Eternity of the World: An Exercise of Faith and Reason. Retrieved April 9, 2007 from http://www2.okbu.edu/academics/natsci/hp/keas/papers/aquinas.htm.

Knight, C. C. (2001). *Wrestling With the Divine: Religion, Science, and Revelation (Theology and the Sciences Series).* Minneapolis, MN: Augsburg Fortress Publishers.

Knitter, P. F. (2002). *Introducing Theologies of Religions.* Maryknoll, NY: Orbis Books.

Koch, C. (2004). *The Quest for Consciousness: A Neurobiological Approach.* Greenwood Village, CO: Roberts & Company Publishers.

Lameter, C. (1997). Divine Action in the Context of Modern Scientific Thinking: Fuller Theological Seminary, Advanced Science and Theology Seminar. Retrieved April 9, 2007 from http://www.apollos.ws/divine-action/.

Lancaster, B. L. (2004). *Approaches to Consciousness: The Marriage of Science and Mysticism* New York, NY: Palgrave Macmillan.

Laszlo, E. (1996) 2nd Revised Ed. *The Systems View of the World: A Holistic Vision for Our Time (Advances in Systems Theory, Complexity, and the Human Sciences).* Cresskill, NJ: Hampton Press.

Laszlo, E., Masulli, I., Artigiani, R., & Csányi, V. (1993). *The Evolution of Cognitive Maps: New Paradigms for the Twenty-First Century.* New York, NY: Routledge-Taylor & Francis Group.

Lawson, E. T. & McCauley, R. N. (1990). *Rethinking Religion: Connecting Cognition and Culture*. New York, NY: Cambridge University Press.

Lerner, M. & Callan, M. (2003). *The Belief in a Just World A Fundamental Delusion (Perspectives in Social Psychology)*. New York, NY: Springer Publishing.

Levy, N. (2007). *Neuroethics: Challenges for the 21st Century*. New York, NY: Cambridge University Press.

Lewis-Williams, D., & Pearce, D. (2005). *Inside the Neolithic Mind: Consciousness, Cosmos, and the Realm of the Gods*. New York, NY: Thames & Hudson.

Lipton, B. (2005). *The Biology of Belief: Unleashing The Power Of Consciousness, Matter And Miracles*. Santa Rosa, CA: Mountain of Love.

Liston, D. D. (1998). Quantum Metaphors and the Study of the Mind-Brain. *The Paidea Project-Twentieth World Congress of Philosophy*. Retrieved April 9, 2007 from http://www.bu.edu/wcp/Papers/Educ/EducList.htm.

Lloyd, Peter B. lectures on Type-type Psycho-Physical Identity: University of Oxford Department for Continuing Education, Undergraduate Philosophy Certificate, and Assignment 8. 1996. http://www.peterblloyd.org/

Lucas, C. (1999). Quantifying Complexity Theory. Retrieved April 9, 2007 from http://www.calresco.org/lucas/quantify.htm.

Madsen, R., Sullivan, W. M., Swidler, A., and Tipton, S. M., (2001). *Meaning and Modernity: Religion, Polity, and Self*. Berkeley, CA: University of California Press.

Malle, B. F. (2006). *How the Mind Explains Behavior: Folk Explanations, Meaning, and Social Interaction*. Cambridge MA: The MIT Press.

Maiello F. (n.d.). Quantum Theory and Metaphysics. Retrieved April 9, 2007 from http://www.geocities.com/egodust/fmpageq.html#QTM.

Mandik, P. (2004). Token Identity Thesis. *Dictionary of Philosophy of Mind*. Retrieved April 9, 2007 from Dictionary of Philosophy: http://philosophy.uwaterloo.ca/MindDict/tokenidentity.html.

Marcus, G. F. (2004). *The Birth of the Mind: How a Tiny Number of Genes Creates the Complexities of Human Thought*. New York, NY: Basic Books.

Marcus, S. J. (Ed.). (2004). *Neuroethics: Mapping the Field*. Washington, DC: Dana Press.

McAdams, D. P. (1997). *The Stories We Live By: Personal Myths and the Making of the Self.* New York, NY: The Guilford Press.

McGrath, A. E. (2004) *The Science Of God: An Introduction To Scientific Theology* Grand Rapids, MI: Wm. B. Eerdmans Publishing Company.

McKinney, L. O. (1994). *Neurotheology: Virtual Religion in the 21st Century.* Cambridge, MA: American Institute for Mindfulness.

Menand, L. (2001). *The Metaphysical Club: A Story of Ideas in America.* New York, NY: Farrar, Straus and Giroux.

Metzinger, T. (Ed.). (2000). *Neural Correlates of Consciousness: Empirical and Conceptual Questions* Cambridge, MA: The MIT Press.

Meyer, J. (1995). *Battlefield of the Mind: Winning the Battle in Your Mind.* Tulsa, Oklahoma: Harrison House, Inc.

Meynell, H. (1997). Hume, Kant, and Rational Theism. *The Telling the Truth Project, Leadership University.* Retrieved April 9, 2007 from http://www.leaderu.com/truth/3truth08.html.

Mithen, S. (1999). *Prehistory of the Mind: The Cognitive Origins of Art, Religion, and Science.* New York, NY: Thames & Hudson.

Moffett, S. (2006). *The Three-Pound Enigma: The Human Brain and the Quest to Unlock Its Mysteries.* Chapel Hill, NC: Algonquin Books.

Moran, L. (1993). What is Evolution? *The Talk Origins Archive.* Retrieved April 9, 2007 from http://www.talkorigins.org/faqs/evolution-definition.html.

Moreland, J.P. (1999). Is Science a Threat or Help to Faith? *Telling the Truth Project, Leadership University.* Retrieved April 9, 2007 from http://www.leaderu.com/real/ri9404/threat.html.

Moser, P.K., & Trout, J.D. (Eds.). (1995). *Contemporary Materialism: A Reader.* New York, NY: Routledge.

Moss, R. A. (1993). *The Brain & the Bible: Is Psychology Compatible with Christianity?* Greenville, SC: Robert A. Moss.

Murphy, G. L. (1996). Possible Influences of Biblical Beliefs upon Physics. Retrieved April 9, 2007 from The American Scientific Affiliation web site: http://www.asa3.org/aSA/PSCF/1996/PSCF6-96Murphy.html.

Murphy, N. & Ellis, G. F. R. (1996). *On the Moral Nature of the Universe - Theology, Cosmology and Ethics.* Minneapolis, MN: Augsburg Press.

Newberg, A., D'Aquili, E., and Rause, V. (2001). *Why God Won't Go Away: Brain Science and the Biology of Belief.* New York, NY: Ballantine Books.

Nicholas, H. (1999). *A History of the Mind: Evolution and the Birth of Consciousness* New York, NY: Springer Publishing.

Nielsen, S. L., Ellis, A., Johnson, W. B. (2001). *Counseling and Psychotherapy With Religious Persons: A Rational Emotive Behavior Therapy Approach (The Lea Series in Personality and Clinical Psychology)* Mahwah, NJ: Lawrence Erlbaum Associates, Inc.

Margolis, H. (1993). *Paradigms and Barriers: How Habits of Mind Govern Scientific Beliefs.* Chicago, IL: University of Chicago Press.

McKinney, M. L. Parker, S. T. (2001). *Origins of Intelligence: The Evolution of Cognitive Development in Monkeys, Apes, and Humans.* Baltimore, MD: The Johns Hopkins University Press.

Pear, J. (2001). *The Science of Learning.* New York, NY: Psychology Press.

Perelman, M. (2005). *Manufacturing Discontent: The Trap of Individualism in Corporate Society.* London, UK: Pluto Press.

Peters, T. (1996). Theology and Science: Where Are We? *ZYGON: Journal of Religion and Science. Vol. 31,* NO. 2.

Peterson, G. R. (2002). *Minding God: Theology and the Cognitive Sciences.* Minneapolis, MN: Augsburg Fortress Publishers.

Peterson, J. (1999). *Maps of Meaning: Architecture of Belief.* New York, NY: Routledge-Taylor & Francis Group.

Piel, G. (2007). *The Age of Science: What Scientists Learned in the Twentieth Century.* New York, NY: Basic Books.

Plate, S. B. (Ed.). (2003) *Representing Religion in World Cinema: Filmmaking, Mythmaking, Culture Making.* New York, NY: Palgrave Macmillan.

Politser, P. (2007). *Neurorationality: A Neuroeconomic Approach to Mental Health and Good Sense.* New York, NY: Oxford University Press USA.

Polkinghorne, J. (1998). *Belief in God in an Age of Science.* New Haven, CT: Yale University Press.

Polkinghorne, J. (1998). *Science & Theology: An Introduction.* Minneapolis, Minnesota: Fortess Press.

Pollack, R. (2000). *The Faith of Biology and The Biology of Faith.* New York, NY: Columbia University Press.

Proudfoot, W. (Ed.). (2004). *William James and a Science of Religions: Reexperiencing the Varieties of Religious Experience (Columbia Series in Science and Religion).* New York, NY: Columbia University Press.

Provenzano, J. & Provenzano, D. DIALOGOS at dialogos@crosswinds. net 10/18/96. Updated: 1998. http://www.proandsons.com/build. pl?header.html+who.html or http://www.proandsons.com/.

Pyysiainen, I., & Anttonen, V. (2002). *Current Approaches in the Cognitive Science of Religion.* New York, NY: Continuum International Publishing Group.

_____. (2003). *How Religion Works: Towards a New Cognitive Science of Religion* Boston, MA: Brill Academic Publishers.

Quantum Theory. (2001-2005). Columbia *Encyclopedia* (6th ed.). Retrieved April 9, 2007 from The Columbia Encyclopedia: http://www.bartleby.com/65/qu/quantumt.html.

Quine, W.V., & Ullian, J.S., (2nd ed.). (1978). *The Web of Belief.* Columbus, OH: McGraw-Hill Humanities/Social Sciences/Languages.

Radin, D. (1997). *The Conscious Universe: The scientific Truth of Psychic Phenomena* New York, NY: Harper Publishing.

Ramachandran, V. S., W. S. Hirstein, K. C. Armel, E. Tecoma, and V. Iragui. 1997. The Neural Basis of Religious Experience. 27th Annual Meeting, New Orleans, LA, 25-30 October 1997. Society for Neuroscience Abstract 23 (2): 519.1.

Randall, J. H. (1977). *The Making of the Modern Mind: A Survey of the Intellectual Background of the Present Age* 50th Anniversary ed. New York, NY: Columbia University Press.

Rappaport, R. A. (1999). *Ritual and Religion in the Making of Humanity (Cambridge Studies in Social and Cultural Anthropology).* New York, NY: Cambridge University Press.

Renvoisé, P. & Morin, C. (2005). *Neuromarketing: Is There a 'Buy Button' in the Brain? Selling to the Old Brain for Instant Success.* San Francisco, CA: SalesBrain. Publishing.

Robbins, W. G. (1984). *Your Brain and the Mind of Christ: A Handbook of Practical Neuroscience for people who want to be like Jesus.* Nashville, TN: Winston-Derek Publishing.

Robinson, B.A. (2000). DEISM: History, Beliefs and Practices. *The Ontario Consultants on Religious Tolerance.* Retrieved April 9, 2007 from http://www.religioustolerance.org/deism.htm.

Robinson, W. (1999). Epiphenomenalism. *Stanford Encyclopedia of Philosophy.* Retrieved April 9, 2007 from the Stanford Encyclopedia of Philosophy: http://plato.stanford.edu/entries/epiphenomenalism/.

Rokeach, M. (1973). *The Opened and Closed Mind: Investigations Into the Nature of Belief Systems and Personality Systems.* New York, NY: Basic Books.

Ruse, M. (2001). *Mystery of Mysteries: Is Evolution a Social Construction?* Cambridge MA, Harvard University Press.

Russell, P. (2000). From Science to Consciousness. In *From Science to God: The Mystery of Consciousness and the Meaning of Light*. (Chapter 1). Retrieved April 9, 2007 from http://www.peterussell.com/sg/contents.php.

Russell, R. J., Murphy, N., & Meyering, T.C., (Eds.). (2000). *Neuroscience and the Person: Scientific Perspectives on Divine Action*. Notre Dame, IN: The University of Notre Dame Press.

Schacter, D. L., & Scarry, E. (Ed.) (1997). *Memory Distortion: How Minds, Brains, and Societies Reconstruct the Past*. Cambridge, MA: Harvard University Press.

_____. & Scarry, E. (Ed.). (2002). *Memory, Brain, and Belief (Mind/ Brain/Behavior Initiative)*. Cambridge, MA: Harvard University Press.

Schleiermacher, F. (1994). Second Speech: On the Essence of Religion. In *On Religion: Speeches to Its Cultured Despisers* (p. 18- 54). (J. Oman, Trans.). Louisville, KY: Westminster John Knox Press. (first published 1799).

Schoepflin, G. L. (1982). Perceptions of the Nature of Science and Christian Strategies for a Science of Nature. *Origins 9(1):*10-27. Retrieved April 9, 2007 from Geoscience Research Institute Webs site: http://www.grisda.org/origins/09010.htm.

Schroeder, G. L. (1998). *The Science of God: The Convergence of Scientific and Biblical Wisdom*. New York, NY: Broadway Books.

_____. (2001). *The Hidden Face of God: Science reveals the Ultimate Truth*. New York, NY: Free Press.

Searle, J. R. (2004). *Mind: A Brief Introduction (Fundamentals of Philosophy Series)* New York, NY: Oxford University Press USA.

Siegel, D. J. (1999). *The Developing Mind: Toward a Neurobiology of Interpersonal Experience* New York, NY: The Guilford Press.

Shermer, M. (2003). *How We Believe: Science, Skepticism, and the Search for God* (2nd ed.). New York, NY: Owl Books.

_____. (2004). *The Science of Good and Evil: Why People Cheat, Share, Gossip, and Follow the Golden Rule* New York, NY: Times Books.

Smart, J. J. C. (2000). The Identity Theory of Mind. (revised 2004). *Stanford Encyclopedia of Philosophy.*Retrieved April 9, 2007 from Stanford Encyclopedia of Philosophy at http://plato.stanford.edu/entries/mindidentity/.

Smith, Q. (1998). Big Bang Cosmology and Atheism: Why the Big Bang is No Help to Theists. [Electronic version]. *Free Inquiry Magazine Vol. 18*, Number 2.

Southgate, C., Deane-Drummond, C., Murray, P., Negus, R., Osborn, L., Poole, M., et al. (1999). *God, Humanity and the Cosmos.* Harrisburg, PA: Trinity Press International.

Spergel, D. N., Hinshaw, G., & Bennett C. L. (1996). The Big Bang Theory. Retrieved April 9, 2007 from http://pdgusers.lbl.gov/-barnett/universe.adventure/big_bang.htm.

Spilka, B., Gorsuch, R., Hood Jr., R. W., & Hunsberger, B., (2003). *The Psychology of Religion, Third Edition: An Empirical Approach* (3rd ed.). New York, NY: The Guilford Press.

Stapp, H. P. (1998). Whiteheadian Process and Quantum Theory of Mind--Paper presented at the Silver Anniversary International Whitehead Conference. Retrieved April 9, 2007 from http://members.aol.com/Mszlazak/WhiteheadQT.html.

Stich, S. (1995). *From Folk Psychology to Cognitive Science: A Case against Belief.* Cambridge, MA: The MIT Press.

Stout, D., & Buddenbaum, J. M. (2001) *Religion and Popular Culture: Studies on the Interaction of Worldviews.* Malden, MA: Blackwell Publishing-Iowa State Press.

Stump, J. (1999). Science, Metaphysics, and Worldviews. *In The Truth Telling Project, Leadership University.* Retrieved April 9, 2007 from http://www.leaderu.com/aip/docs/stump.html.

Swimme, B. & Berry, T. (1994). *The Universe Story: A Celebration of the Unfolding of the Cosmos.* New York, NY: Harper Publishing.

Swinburne, R. G. (2002). The Justification of Theism. *The Telling the Truth Telling Project, Leadership University.* Retrieved April 9, 2007 from http://www.leaderu.com/truth/3truth09.html.

Synan, V. (2001). *The Century of the Holy Spirit: 100 Years of Pentecostal and Charismatic Renewal.* Nashville, TN: Thomas Nelson Publishers.

Tarnas, R. (1993). *The Passion of the Western Mind: Understanding the Ideas that Have Shaped Our World View.* New York, NY: Ballantine Books- Random House Publishing Group.

Taylor, K. (2004). *Brainwashing: The Science of Thought Control.* New York, NY: Oxford University Press USA.

Theism. (2007). In *Encyclopedia Britannica Online.* Retrieved April 9, 2007 from Encyclopedia Britannica Online: http://www.britannica.com/ebc/article-9380558

Theosophy (1940). Origins of Scientific Materialism. *Theosophy Vol. 28*, No. 12, October, 1940. Retrieved April 9, 2007 from: http://www.wisdomworld.org/setting/materialism.html.

Thomas, D. (1996). Rudiments of Quantum Theory. Retrieved April 9, 2007 from http://www.cobalt.chem.ucalgary.ca/ziegler/educmat/chm386/rudiment/rudiment.htm.

Trull, D. (n.d.). The God Spot. *Enigma*. Retrieved April 9, 2007 from http://cas.bellarmine.edu/tietjen/Human%20Nature%20S%201999/Creationism/is_the_human_mind_touched_by_god.htm.

Turner, M. (2003). *Cognitive Dimensions of Social Science: The Way We Think About Politics, Economics, Law, and Society* (new edited ed.). New York, NY: Oxford University Press, USA.

Turner, W. (2007). METAPHYSICS. *New Advent Catholic Encyclopedia*. Retrieved April 9, 2007 from New Advent Catholic Encyclopedia: http://www.newadvent.org/cathen/10226a.htm#1.

Turrell, D. (2004). *Science vs. Religion: The 500-year War, Finding God in the Heat of the Battle*. Frederick, MD: PublishAmerica.

Ulanov, A. & Ulanov, B. (1975). *Religion and the Unconscious*. Philadelphia, PA: The Westminster Press.

Van Gelder, T. J. (1998). Monism, Dualism, Pluralism. *Mind and Language, Vol. 13*, 76-97. Retrieved April 9, 2007 from http://www.philosophy.unimelb.edu.au/tgelder/papers/MDP.pdf.

Velmans, M. (1997). Defining Consciousness. Retrieved April 9, 2007 from faculty page of Professor Max Velmans, Department of Psychology, Goldsmiths University of London, web site: http://www.goldsmiths.ac.uk/departments/psychology/staff/velpub.html.

Vyse, S. A. (2000). *Believing in Magic: The Psychology of Superstition*. New York, NY: Oxford University Press USA.

Watson, P. (2002). *The Modern Mind: An Intellectual History of the 20th Century*. New York, NY: Harper Perennial.

Welch, E. T. (1998). *Blame It on the Brain: Distinguishing Chemical Imbalances, Brain Disorders, and Disobedience*. Phillipsburg, NJ: P & R Publishing.

Whitehouse, H. (2004). *Modes of Religiosity: A Cognitive Theory of Religious Transmission (Cognitive Science of Religion)*. Lanham, MD: Alta Mira Press.

_____. (2004). *Theorizing Religions Past: Archaeology, History, and Cognition (Cognitive Science of Religion Series)*. Lanham, MD: Alta Mira Press.

_____., & McCauley, R. N. (Eds.). (2005). *Mind and Religion: Psychological and Cognitive Foundations of Religion: Psychological and Cognitive Foundations of Religion (Cognitive Science of Religion)*. Lanham, MD: Alta Mira Press.

Wilson, R. A. (2004). *Boundaries of the Mind: The Individual in the Fragile Sciences*. New York, NY: Cambridge University Press.

Wolfe, A. (2005). *The Transformation of American Religion: How We Actually Live Our Faith*. Chicago, IL: University of Chicago Press.

Wozniak, R. H. (1992). Mind and Body: René Descartes to William James. *Serendip*. Retrieved April 9, 2007 from http://serendip.brynmawr.edu/Mind/Table.html.

Young, R. M. Mind, Brain and Adaptation in the Nineteenth Century: Cerebral Localization and Its Biological Context from Gall to Ferrier. *Human Nature Review*. Retrieved April, 9 2007 from http://human-nature.com/mba/mba1.html.

Zachar, P. (2004). Physicalism. *Dictionary of Philosophy of Mind*. Retrieved April 9, 2007 from the Dictionary of Philosophy of Mind: http://philosophy.uwaterloo.ca/MindDict/physicalism.html.

Additional Resources

(According to Subject Areas)

Biology:

Benson, Herbert, and Marg Stark. (1996). *Timeless Healing: The Power and Biology of Belief.*

Buckman, Robert. (2002). *Can We Be Good Without God?: Biology, Behavior, and the Need to Believe.*

Carey, Susan, and Rochel Gelman. (1991). *The Epigenesis of Mind: Essays on Biology and Cognition (Jean Piaget Symposia Series).*

Clark, Stephen R. (2000). *Biology and Christian Ethics (New Studies in Christian Ethics)*

Falk, Darrel R., and Francis Collins. (2004). *Coming to Peace With Science: Bridging the Worlds Between Faith and Biology.*

Grene, Marjorie, and David Depew. (2004). *The Philosophy of Biology: An Episodic History (The Evolution of Modern Philosophy).*

Hull, David L., and Michael Ruse. (1998). *The Philosophy of Biology (Oxford Readings in Philosophy).*

Lipton, Bruce H. (2005). *The Biology of Belief: Unleashing The Power Of Consciousness, Matter And Miracles.* Santa Rosa, CA: Mountain of Love.

_____. (2006). *The Wisdom of Your Cells: How Your Beliefs Control Your Biology.*

Giovannoli, J. & Wilson, D.A. (2001). *The Biology of Belief: How Our Biology Biases Our Beliefs and Perceptions.* info@rosettapress. com: Rosetta Press.

Lennox, James G. (2000). *Aristotle's Philosophy of Biology: Studies in the Origins of Life Science (Cambridge Studies in Philosophy and Biology).*

Newberg, Andrew, and Mark Robert Waldman. (2006). *Why We Believe What We Believe: Uncovering Our Biological Need for Meaning, Spirituality, and Truth.*

Pollack, R. (2000). *The Faith of Biology and The Biology of Faith*. New York, NY: Columbia University Press

Rottschaefer, William Andrew. (2003). *The Biology and Psychology of Moral Agency (Cambridge Studies in Philosophy and Biology)*.

Trusted, Jennifer. (2005). *Beliefs and Biology: Theories of Life and Living, Second Edition*

Wright, Richard T. (1989). *Biology through the Eyes of Faith*. New York, NY: HarperCollins Publishers.

Chemistry:

Austin, J.H. (1999). *Zen and the Brain: Towards An Understanding of Meditation and Consciousness*. Cambridge, Massachusetts: The MIT Press

Bhushan, Nalini, and Stuart Rosenfeld. (2006). *Of Minds and Molecules: New Philosophical Perspectives on Chemistry*.

Cognitive Science:

Andresen, J. & Forman, R.K.C. (Eds.). (2000). *Cognitive Models and Spiritual Maps: Interdisciplinary Exploration of Religious Experience (Journal of Consciousness Studies)* Charlottesville, VA: Imprint Academic.

Boyer, P. (1994). *The Naturalness of Religious Ideas: A Cognitive Theory of Religion*. Berkeley: University of California Press

Chakrabarti, Kisor Kumar. (1999). *Classical Indian Philosophy of Mind: The Nyaya Dualist Tradition*. New York, NY: State University of New York Press.

Gardner, Howard. 2004. *Changing Minds: The Art and Science of Changing Our Own and Other People's Minds*. Boston, MA: Harvard Business School Press.

_____. 1985. *The Mind's New Science: A History of Cognitive Revolution*. New York, NY: Basic Books.

Mithen, S. (1999). *Prehistory of the Mind: The Cognitive Origins of Art, Religion, and Science*. New York, NY: Thames & Hudson.

Peterson, G. R. (2002). *Minding God: Theology and the Cognitive Sciences*. Minneapolis, MN: Augsburg Fortress Publishers.

Pyysiainen, I., & Anttonen, V. (2002). *Current Approaches in the Cognitive Science of Religion*. New York, NY: Continuum International Publishing Group.

_____. (2003). *How Religion Works: Towards a New Cognitive Science of Religion* Boston, MA: Brill Academic Publishers.

Russell, John Robert, et al. (1999). Neuroscience and the Person: Scientific Perspectives on Divine Action. Vatican Observatory Foundation.

Stich, S. (1995). *From Folk Psychology to Cognitive Science: A Case against Belief.* Cambridge, MA: The MIT Press.

Turner, M. (2003). *Cognitive Dimensions of Social Science: The Way We Think About Politics, Economics, Law, and Society* (new edited ed.). New York, NY: Oxford University Press, USA.

Varela, Francisco J, et al. (2000). *The Embodied Mind: Cognitive Science and Human Experience.* Cambridge, MA: The MIT Press.

Whitehouse, H. (2004). *Modes of Religiosity: A Cognitive Theory of Religious Transmission (Cognitive Science of Religion).* Lanham, MD: Alta Mira Press.

Whitehouse, H. & McCauley, R. N. (Eds.). (2005). *Mind and Religion: Psychological and Cognitive Foundations of Religion: Psychological and Cognitive Foundations of Religion (Cognitive Science of Religion).* Lanham, MD: Alta Mira Press.

Economics:

Glimcher, Paul W. (2004). *Decisions, Uncertainty, and the Brain: The Science of Neuroeconomics.* Cambridge, MA: The MIT Press.

Montague. (2006). *Value, Money, And Belief: Turning Feelings into Numbers in the New Age of Neuroscience.*

Renvoisé, P. & Morin, C. (2005). *Neuromarketing: Is There a 'Buy Button' in the Brain? Selling to the Old Brain for Instant Success.* San Francisco, CA: SalesBrain. Publishing.

Engineering:

Vick, Steven G. (2002). *Degrees of Belief: Subjective Probability and Engineering Judgment.*

Ethics:

Clifford, William Klingdon, and Timothy J. Madigan. (1999). *The Ethics of Belief and Other Essays (Great Books in Philosophy).*

Gazzaniga, M. S. (2005). *The Ethical Brain.* Washington, DC: Dana Press

Glannon, W. (2007). *Defining Right and Wrong in Brain Science: Essential Readings in Neuroethics.* Washington DC: Dana Press.

Illes, J. (Ed.). (2005). *Neuroethics: Defining the Issues in Theory, Practice and Policy.* New York, NY: Oxford University Press USA.

Levy, N. (2007). *Neuroethics: Challenges for the 21st Century.* New York, NY: Cambridge University Press.

Marcus, S. J. (Ed.). (2004). *Neuroethics: Mapping the Field.* Washington, DC: Dana Press.

Genetics:

Avise, john C. (2001). *The Genetic Gods: Evolution and Belief in Human Affairs.*

Hamer, D. (2005). *The God Gene: How Faith is Hardwired into Our Genes.* New York, NY: Anchor Books.

Marcus, G. F. (2004). *The Birth of the Mind: How a Tiny Number of Genes Creates the Complexities of Human Thought.* New York, NY: Basic Books.

Meister, Chad V. (2006) *Building Belief: Constructing Faith from the Ground Up.*

History:

Knight, David M., and Matthew D. Eddy. (2005). *Science And Beliefs: From Natural Philosophy To Natural Science, 1700-1900 (Science, Technology and Culture, 1700-1945)*

Neuroscience:

Albright, C. & Ashbrook, J. (2001). *Where God Lives in the Human Brain* (2nd ed.). Naperville, IL: Sourcebooks Inc.

Alper, M. (2000). *The "God" Part of the Brain: A Scientific Interpretation of Human Spirituality and God* (5th ed.). New York: Rogue Press

Ashbrook, J. B., & Albright, C. R. (1997). *The Humanizing Brain: Where Religion and Neuroscience Meet.* Cleveland, OH: The Pilgrim Press.

Bennett, M. R., and P.M.S. Hacker. (2003). *Philosophical Foundations of Neuroscience.*

Bulkeley, Kelly. (2005). *Soul, Psyche, Brain: New Directions in the Study of Religion and Brain-Mind Science.*

Connolly, W. E. (2002). *Neuropolitics: Thinking, Culture, Speed (Theory Out of Bounds, Number 23).* Minneapolis, MN: University of Minnesota Press.

Cory Jr., G. A. (2003). *The Consilient Brain: The Bioneurological Basis of Economics, Society, and Politics.* (2nd. ed.). New York, NY: Springer Publishing.

Chakrabarti, K. K. (1999). *Classical Indian Philosophy of Mind: The Nyaya Dualist Tradition.* Albany, NY: State University of New York Press.

Dalai Lama. (1999). *Consciousness at the Crossroads: Conversations with the Dalai Lama on Brain Science and Buddhism.* Ithaca NY: Snow Lion Publications.

Dalton, C. W. (1990). *The Right Brian and Religion: A Discussion of Religion in the Context of the Right and Left Brain Theory.* Lakeside, CA: Big Blue Books.

D'Aquili, E., & Newberg, A. (1999). *The Mystical Mind: Probing the Biology of Religious Experience, Theology and the Sciences.* Minneapolis, MN: Augsburg

Damasio, Antonio. (2003). *Looking for Spinoza: Joy, Sorrow and the Feeling Brain.* Orlando, FL: Harcourt, Inc.

deCharms, Christopher. (1998). *Two Views of Mind: Abhidharma and Brain Science.* Ithaka, NY: Snow Lion Publications.

Joseph, R., Newberg, A., Albright, C.R., James, W., Nietzsche, F., & Persinger, M. (2003). *Neurotheology: Brain, Science, Spirituality, Religious Experience* (2nd ed.). Lanham, MD: University Press.

Lane, Richard D., and Lynn Nadel. (2002). *Cognitive Neuroscience of Emotion (Series in Affective Science).*

Larsen, Jerry. (2000). *Religious Education and the Brain: A Practical Resource for Understanding How We Learn about God.* New York, NY: Paulist Press.

McGraw, John. (2004). *Brain & Belief: An Exploration of the Human Soul.*

Nelson, Charles A., et al. (2006). *Neuroscience of Cognitive Development: The Role of Experience and the Developing Brain.*

Newberg, A., D'Aquili, E., and Rause, V. (2001). *Why God Won't Go Away: Brain Science and the Biology of Belief.* New York, NY: Ballantine Books.

Persinger, Michael A. 1987. *Neuropsychological Bases of God Beliefs.* New York: Praeger.

Politser, P. (2007). *Neurorationality: A Neuroeconomic Approach to Mental Health and Good Sense.* New York, NY: Oxford University Press USA.

Robbins, W. G. (1984). *Your Brain and the Mind of Christ: A Handbook of Practical Neuroscience for people who want to be like Jesus.* Nashville, TN: Winston-Derek Publishing.

Russell, R. J., Murphy, N., & Meyering, T.C., (Eds.). (2000). *Neuroscience and the Person: Scientific Perspectives on Divine Action.* Notre Dame, IN: The University of Notre Dame Press.

Schlagel, Richard H. (2001). *The Vanquished Gods: Science, Religion, and the Nature of Belief (Prometheus Lecture Series).*

Sitze, Bob, and Robert Sylwester. (2004). *Your Brain Goes To Church: Neuroscience and Congregational Life.*

Szasz, Thomas S. (2002). *The Meaning of Mind: Language, Morality, and Neuroscience.*

Tancredi, Laurence. (2005). *Hardwired Behavior: What Neuroscience Reveals about Morality.*

Wallace, B. Allan. (2006). *Contemplative Science: Where Buddhism And Neuroscience Converge (Columbia Series in Science and Religion).*

Wallace, B. Allan, et al. (1999). *Consciousness at the Crossroads: Conversations with THE DALAI LAMA on Brain Science and Buddhism.* Ithaka, NY: Snow Lion Publications.

Philosophy:

Bechtel, William, et al. (2001). *Philosophy and the Neurosciences: A Reader.*

Physics:

Butterfield, Jeremy. (2006). *Philosophy of Physics (Handbook of the Philosophy of Science) 2 volume set.*

Cushing James T. (2006). *Philosophical Concepts in Physics: The Historical Relation between Philosophy and Scientific Theories.*

Davies, Paul. (1984). *God and the New Physics.*

DiSalle, Robert. (2006). *Understanding Space-Time: The Philosophical Development of Physics from Newton to Einstein.*

Geis, Jack W. (2003). *Physics, Metaphysics and God.*

Hodgson, Peter E. (2006). *Theology and Modern Physics (Ashgate Science and Religion Series).*

Kragh, Helge. (2002). *Quantum Generations: A History of Physics in the Twentieth Century.*

Jammer, Max. (2002). *Einstein and Religion: Physics and Theology.*

Jones, Marie D. (2006). *PSIence: How New Discoveries in Quantum Physics and New Science May Explain the Existence of Paranormal Phenomena.*

Polkinghorne, John. (1998). *Belief in God in an Age of Science.* New Haven, CT: Yale University Press.

———————. (1998). *Science and Theology: An Introduction.* Minneapolis, MN: Fortress Press.

Tuszynski, Jack A. (2006). *The Emerging Physics of Consciousness (The Frontiers Collection).*

Politics:

Blank, Robert H. (1999). *Brain Policy: How the New Neuroscience Will Change Our Lives and Our Politics.*

Goertzel, T. (1992) *Turncoats & True Believers: The Dynamics of Political Belief and Disillusionment.* Amherst, NY: Prometheus Books.

Psychology:

Belgrave, Faye Z., and Kevin W. Allison. (2005). *African American Psychology: From Africa to America.*

Bynum, E. B. (1999). *The African Unconsciousness: Roots of Ancient Mysticism and Modern Psychology.* New York, NY: Teachers College Press.

Beit-Hallahmi, B., & Argyle, M. (1997). *The Psychology of Religious Behaviors, Belief & Experience.* New York: Routledge-Taylor & Francis Group

Carter, Rita. (1999). *Mapping the Mind.* Los Angeles, CA: University of California Press.

Dowd, E. Thomas, and Stevan Lars Nielsen. (2006) *The Psychologies in Religion: Working With the Religious Client.*

Faber, M. D. (2004). *The Psychological Roots Of Religious Belief: Searching For Angels And The Parent-god.*

Gendlin, Eugene. (1962/1997). *Experiencing and the Creation of Meaning: A Philosophical and Psychological Approach to the Subjective.* Evanston, Illinois: Northwestern University Press.

Francis, L. J. (2005). *Faith and Psychology: Personality, Religion and the Individual.* Nashville, TN: Abingdon Press.

Fuller, A. R. (1994). *Psychology & Religion: Eight Points of View.* (3rd ed). Lanham, MD: Rowman & Littlefield Publishers, Inc.

Hilliard III, A. G. (1998). *The Reawakening of the African Mind* (revised ed.). Gainesville, FL: Makare Publishing.

Horton, R. (1997). *Patterns of Thought in Africa and the West: Essays on Magic, Religion and Science.* New York, NY: Cambridge University Press.

James, William. (1994/1902). *The Varieties of Religious Experience.* New York, NY: Modern Library-Random House Publishing.

Langer, Ellen J. (1997). *The Power of Mindful Learning.* Cambridge, MA: Perseus Publishing.

—————. (1989). *Mindfulness.* Reading, MA: Addison-Wesley Publishing Company.

Mc Ginn, Colin. (1999). *The Mysterious Flame: Conscious Minds in A Material World.* New York, NY: Basic Books.

Moss, R. A. (1993). *The Brain & the Bible: Is Psychology Compatible with Christianity?* Greenville, SC: Robert A. Moss.

Nisbett, Richard E. (2003). *The Geography of Thought: How Asians and Westerners Think Differently...and Why*. New York, NY: Free Press.

Pratt, James Bissett. (2006). *The Psychology Of Religious Belief*.

Spilka, B., Gorsuch, R., Hood Jr., R. W., & Hunsberger, B., (2003). *The Psychology of Religion, Third Edition: An Empirical Approach* (3rd ed.). New York, NY: The Guilford Press.

Vyse, S. A. (2000). *Believing in Magic: The Psychology of Superstition*. New York, NY: Oxford University Press USA.

Wegner, Daniel M. (2002). *The Illusion of Conscious Will*. Cambridge, MA: The MIT Press.

Welch, Edward T. 1998. *Blame It on the Brain: Distinguishing Chemical Imbalances, Brain Disorders, and Disobedience*. Phillipsburg, NJ: P & R Publishing.

Whitehouse, H. & McCauley, R. N. (Eds.). (2005). *Mind and Religion: Psychological and Cognitive Foundations of Religion: Psychological and Cognitive Foundations of Religion (Cognitive Science of Religion)*. Lanham, MD: Alta Mira Press.

Religion:

Brown, Kevin, et al. (2001). *Evolution and Baha'i Belief: Abdu'l-Baha's Response to Nineteenth Century Darwinism (Studies in the Babi and Baha'i Religions, V. 12)*.

Godlove, T.F. (1989). *Religion, Interpretation, and the Diversity of Belief: The Framework Model from Kant to Durkheim to Davidson*. Cambridge: Cambridge University press.

Jacobs, L. (1992). *Religion and the Individual : A Jewish Perspective (Cambridge Studies in Religious Traditions)*. New York, NY: Cambridge University Press.

McVeigh, Brian J. (1997). *Spirits, Selves, and Subjectivity in a Japanese New Religion: The Cultural Psychology of Belief in Shukyo Mahikari (Studies in Asian Thought and Religion)*.

Beliefs (General):

Dodd, Ray. (2004). *The Power of Belief: Essential Tools for an Extraordinary Life*.

Frijda, Nico H., et al. (2006). *Emotions and Beliefs: How Feelings Influence Thoughts (Studies in Emotion and Social Interaction)*.

Miller, Lloyd D. (2006). *Belief, that Tricky Business.*

Poole. (1995). *Beliefs and Values in Science Education (Developing Science and Technology Education)*

Rubin, Kenneth H. (2006). *Parenting Beliefs, Behaviors, and Parent-Child Relations: A Cross-Cultural Perspective.*

Wright, Lorraine M., et al. (2001). *Beliefs and Families: A Model for Healing Illness (Families & Health).*

664732

Made in the USA